20% Dis

NOURISHING THE LIBERTY TREE

To Carmel, a brave and beautiful sister

NOURISHING THE LIBERTY TREE

LABOUR POLITICS IN LEEDS, 1880–1914

Tom Woodhouse

KEELEUNIVERSITY**PRESS**

First published in 1996 by
Keele University Press
Keele, Staffordshire

© Tom Woodhouse

Composed by KUP
Printed on acid-free paper
by Hartnolls, Bodmin,
Cornwall, England

ISBN 1 85331 165 0

Contents

List of tables

Abbreviations

ASCJ	Amalgamated Society of Carpenters and Joiners
ASE	Amalgamated Society of Engineers
ASLEF	Amalgamated Society of Locomotive Engineers and Firemen
AST	Amalgamated Society of Tailors
BSP	British Socialist Party
GGLU	Gasworkers' and General Labourers' Union
ILP	Independent Labour Party
IRC	Industrial Remuneration Conference
LEL	Labour Electoral League
LEU	Labour Electoral Union
LICS	Leeds Industrial Co-operative Society
LLRC	Leeds Labour Representation Committee
LRC	Labour Representation Committee
LSRU	Leeds Social Reform Union
LTC	Leeds Trades Council
LWMA	Leeds Working Men's Association
NLRC	National Labour Representation Committee
NUBSO	National Union of Boot and Shoe Operatives
SDF	Social Democratic Federation
TC	Trades Council
TUC	Trades Union Congress
YFT	Yorkshire Factory Times
YFTC	Yorkshire Federation of Trades Councils
YLL	Yorkshire Labour League

Acknowledgements

Thanks are due to many people who helped and motivated me at various times. James O'Connell supported me from the start, with that first sabbatical many years ago. Colleagues in the Peace Studies Department, especially Malcolm Dando, Paul Rogers, and Oliver Ramsbotham have been consistently encouraging. Old friends who know the field of labour and social history better than I – (Tom Steele, Vince Di Girolamo, John Quail and Bernie Stinson). Andrew Richardson for patient and fast word-processing. Geoffrey Redfearn, whose sharp pen and clear mind cut out (painlessly) so much of the fat.

Gill, Tim and Jenny for bearing with the absences. And Weetwood School Class 6 boys football team in Leeds for being so damn good!

Introduction

… the West Riding woollen district, in the 1880s, was a distinctive community, with common characteristics imposed by its staple industries, geographical isolation, and historical traditions …

In such communities, an 'alien agitator' from outside would make little headway: but once the local leaders moved the whole community might follow. Leeds, on the eastern edge of the woollen district, was a more cosmopolitan city … New ideas, new national movements, tended to extend their influence to the woollen districts, not directly from London but by way of Leeds; the textile workers' leaders learnt their socialism from the Leeds and Bradford Socialist Leagues; Ben Turner, the dialect poet from Huddersfield, was initiated into the movement when he 'flitted' for two years to Leeds.

Edward Thompson in 'Homage to Tom Maguire'.[1]

Leeds too had the geographical advantage of being centrally located at the crossroads of major road, rail, and canal communications, in a fiercely independent county proud of its difference. Through its textile manufacturing it was also more dependent on women's labour and their early militancy and unionisation suggested alternatives to domestic servility. It was a major financial centre dependent on 'mental labour'. It bore an historic burden. Its ageing nineteenth century's Liberal elite's gestures towards civic consciousness seemed like a task in need of completion.

Tom Steele on Leeds and the work of Orage and
the Leeds Arts Club, early twentieth century.[2]

The economic and industrial history of cities like Leeds is usually much better known than the history of those political ideas which from time to time aroused the passions of their inhabitants. Leeds engineers, such as Matthew Murray, Peter Fairbairn and James Kitson, produced machinery which was nationally and internationally regarded. John Barran established the ready-made clothing industry in the town, and the businesses of Hepworths and Burtons made the name of Leeds virtually synonymous with this industry worldwide. The city even claims distinction as the place where the Marks and Spencer retail chain originated, beginning as a penny stall in Leeds market. It might even claim to have been a pioneer of the modern cinema, because it was in Leeds in 1888 that Louis Le Prince made the world's first moving pictures when he filmed traffic coming over Leeds Bridge.

Leeds never became a one-industry town and an immensely varied economy is one of its distinctive characteristics. It is different from the woollen-district towns to its West: it is bigger in population than any other town in West Yorkshire and, with its role as a regional centre offering commercial, distribution, retail, marketing, managerial and transport facilities, 'it has always been far more cosmopolitan, far more dependent on migrants, and perhaps far more anonymous than its neighbours'.[3]

Leeds, then, has for a long time been a place where not only goods but also people passed through, a place, as Fraser describes it, of comers and goers, a melting pot.[4] As the combined effects of industrialization and urbanization created a society divided economically and geographically along class lines, the years of Chartist activity were ones of intense debate about how the separate classes could co-exist peacefully and how the wealth of the new industrial society might be shared more equitably or generated differently. In the 1830s and 1840s it was described as 'an emporium of social ideas'. Leeds was a centre for radical ideas which affected the rest of the region, as well as impacting on national politics, yet its politics was influenced, inevitably, by its economy and its complex social structure. While Leeds had a strong radical tradition, it never became a place dominated by working-class political interests and organizations in the way that, for example, Bradford and Sheffield did. It was a city that, during the years covered by this book, bridged the utilitarian industrial concerns of mid-Victorian England while at the same time anticipating the new ways of thinking of the twentieth century. As Tom Steele, writing of the role of a provincial avant-garde in the city, has said: 'something of significance was happening in Leeds during these years ... [and] new theories and practices were produced rather than consumed'.[5]

This book sets out to explore labour, radical and socialist politics in Leeds, which was a centre for the cultivation and dissemination of ideas about society and politics as much as it was the industrial and commercial capital of the West Riding of Yorkshire. The period covered is between the years 1880 and 1914 when, just as had occurred in the Chartist period forty or fifty years previously, the values and ideas of industrial society were challenged once again in a ferment of new thinking about social, political, and economic issues. The old problem of how best to place the 'unbound Prometheus' under democratic control emerged again, and a radical political subculture flourished, containing a wide spectrum of opinion, ranging from those who wished to establish a revolutionary socialist commonwealth through to those who sought pragmatic reform. Out of this ferment, the modern Labour Party was established as a broad church or labour alliance, seeking to combine the objectives of social reform through Parliament with an ethic or sentiment of socialist fellowship which had both working- and middle-class support.

What happened in Leeds, of course, has to be interpreted in the context of what went on elsewhere. The way in which we understand British labour history in particular and British history in general has been considerably developed in the last two decades by the flourishing of local and regional studies. Much of the stimulus for this came from the seminal work of historians like Asa Briggs, Edward Thompson, and J. F. C. Harrison, whose work inspired a new generation of labour historians,[6] including myself, to explore the way in which labour politics, rooted in the concerns of local communities, was capable of impacting on the national political scene. Derek Fraser's *A History of Modern Leeds* provides an excellent survey of the general economic, political and social development of Leeds between 1700 and recent times. For West Yorkshire in general, the work of Reynolds, Laybourn, James and Jowitt, in particular, has made an enormous contribution to our understanding of how labour and local politics changed during the period covered by this book and the contribution to that change made by people and places in West Yorkshire. The *Centennial History of the Independent Labour Party* published in 1992, Reynolds' and Laybourn's *Liberalism and the Rise of Labour, 1880–1914*, and Steele's *Alfred Orage and the Leeds Arts Club, 1893–1923* provide important treatments of the influence of the West Yorkshire region on the modernization of British politics and ideas which occurred in the early years of this century.[7]

Edward Thompson's 'Homage to Tom Maguire' was an inspirational essay on socialist ideas and the emergence of the Independent Labour Party (ILP) in Leeds in the 1880s and 1890s. Equally, in his brilliant *The Making of the English Working Class*, he wrote of the 'Planting of the Liberty Tree', when ordinary people struggled to democratize the forces of industrialism.[8] In this book I examine how a generation of people who had benefited from the realization of that earlier dream, by enjoying the benefits of formal democracy, i.e. the right to vote, tried to nourish the liberty tree in their own time. The organization of the book is both chronological and thematic. The first chapter looks at the pre-socialist phase of labour politics, roughly from 1867 to the mid-1880s, when liberal ideas dominated labour thinking. The second chapter shows how liberal assumptions and the political support of the labour movement were beginning to become less certain by the early 1890s. Chapter three deals with the revival of socialist thinking and activity in Leeds with the formation of the Social Democratic Federation (SDF) and the

Socialist League in the mid-1880s, and how these organizations developed to influence the emergence of the ILP. The ILP is covered in chapter four, and its influence on the formation of the Labour Party and the progress of that party is the subject of chapter five. Throughout the book there is a concern with two overarching themes: one relates to the relationship between liberalism and labour, and between the Liberal Party and the Labour Party. The other is a concern with the relationship between industrial society, politics and democracy. Both these themes are brought together in the final chapter, which assesses the achievements of the Labour Party and the 'suppressed alternatives' with which the party conducted a discourse about the vital issues of economic and political democracy.

Notes

1. E. P. Thompson, 'Homage to Tom Maguire', in A. Briggs and J. Saville (eds), *Essays in Labour History* (London, 1967), pp. 279–80.
2. Tom Steele, *Alfred Orage and the Leeds Arts Club 1893–1923* (Aldershot, 1990), p. 263.
3. D. Fraser, 'Modern Leeds: A Postscript', in D. Fraser (ed.), *A History of Modern Leeds* (Manchester, 1980), p. 465.
4. *Ibid.*, p. 469.
5. Steele, *Alfred Orage*, p. 19.
6. Their work in relation to Leeds and Yorkshire is listed in the bibliography.
7. Steele, *Alfred Orage*; K. Laybourn and J. Reynolds, *Liberalism and the Rise of Labour, 1880–1914* (London, 1984); D. James, T. Jowitt and K. Laybourn (eds), *The Centennial History of the Independent Labour Party* (Halifax, 1992).
8. E. P. Thompson, *The Making of the English Working Class* (London, 1968).

Chapter 1

Trade Unions, Radical Liberals and the Ethic of Co-operation

On every side class and class are becoming more separated, distinct and antagonistic so far as capital and labour are concerned. The growing intelligence of the rising generation will make this antagonism the more fatal ... We therefore turn to the consideration of which the professors of Christianity preach or profess and which the practical philosophers of the day ignore ... viz, the unity of general interests as the best way of advancing the individual ... Charity leaves all the sources of the evil still existing, and communism destroys individual motives to exertion. Latterly a system of distributing equivalently has been suggested, and to some extent applied, under the name of co-operation.

Leeds Express, 14 January 1865.

The labour movement: trade unions

Labour politics between 1880 and 1914 cannot be understood without some reference to the structure and ideas of the labour movement in the decades which preceded the 1880s. In the third quarter of the century the issue of power and conflict in industrial society, and the 'labour question' that it raised, was regarded on all sides as a vital one. It was recognized by Liberal opinion that, after the second Reform Act of 1867, not only the political future of Leeds Liberalism but the whole broader question of industrial and economic relations were dependant upon a satisfactory resolution of the labour question. The quality of debate about the role of labour in society was carried on at times to a very high level indeed, and with a detachment and depth of perception not often encountered in the West Riding in later years. The question was to take on a larger political significance as the franchise was progressively extended and the basis for mass democratic politics established. The Reform Act of 1867 gave the parliamentary vote to male householders living in parliamentary boroughs, and the third Reform Act of 1884 conferred it upon male householders in county constituencies. In 1882 working men were enabled to become representatives in local government, when the property qualifications for local councillors and aldermen was abolished. Although it is true that the formal completion of the democratic franchise cannot be said to have been achieved until the Acts of 1918 and 1928 included adult men and women, the Acts of the 1860s and 1880s, along with the secret ballot introduced in an Act of 1871, effectively created an urban electorate of whom the majority were working men. The work of historians such as Edward Thompson and J. F. C. Harrison has shown how the common people of West Yorkshire participated in 'planting the liberty tree' which ultimately enabled this democratic development to occur.[1]

After the Chartist period, the shape of the Leeds labour movement came into focus in the 1860s as a result of the attentions of radical Liberals, who wished to bring the labour vote that was created after 1867 as much as possible into the Liberal Party fold.[2] Two of these Liberal Party 'missionaries' visited Leeds, and reported that:

> ... the increase in Leeds is enormous. The old register was only 8,480 while the new one will be a little over 38,000. This extraordinary addition is principally composed of mechanics and factory workers, or as they are termed here 'mill hands'. There has been no gauge taken of their opinions, but they are believed to be Liberal ... The Trades Societies are both numerous and strong, and will be useful for working ...[3]

In 1868 the labour movement was composed of small, exclusive, craft societies, representing the attitudes of the organized artisans of the town. According to a report for the Reform League, the trades that were organized in Leeds in the late 1860s were as shown in Table 1.

The organized working class of Leeds was represented by a relatively small group of trade societies, with approximately 3,600 members. Of these trade-unionists, 44 per cent belonged to predominantly local trade societies, while the largest single organized trade was represented by the Amalgamated Society of Engineers (ASE), which, with a total of approximately 1,300 members, itself accounted for one-third of the trade-union movement in the town. In 1870 only 1.2 per cent of the population of Leeds were members of trade unions. By 1892 the figure had expanded to 3.85 per cent. In relation to the occupied population, the proportions were, of course, higher: in 1870 around 3.9 per cent, and in 1892, 9.4 per cent.[4] These trade unions formed what has been called an aristocracy of labour. Their rulebooks, objectives and activities made it clear that they did not have any of the grand ambitions for social transformation shown by the working-class movements in the first half of the century. They did not claim to act on behalf of working people in general. John Burnett, the labour correspondent of the Board of Trade, believed that they represented, and should, indeed, only represent, the best and most able of the working class: 'They cannot by any means be said to include within

Table 1   Trades organized in Leeds, 1868

Membership	Trades
Under 50	Tin-plate workers
	Corn millers
	Coopers
	Glass-bottle makers
	Lithographers
	Boiler-makers
	Heavy-engine makers
	Curriers
	Upholsterers
	Bakers
	Cabinet-makers
	Old cordwainers
50–100	Brass-founders
	Flax and hemp dressers
	Cloth dressers
	Brush-makers
	General Union of Carpenters
	Stonemasons
	Boot and shoe riveters
100–200	Blacksmiths
	Cloth pressers
	Hammermen (2 branches)
	Iron-founders
	Painters
	Plasterers
Above 200	Amalgamated Society of Carpenters and Joiners (215: 2 branches)
	Amalgamated Society of Engineers (1,329: 5 branches)

Source: Reform League, *Report on Leeds*, 1868.

their ranks anything like the great body of workers within the kingdom, but there is little doubt their members are the flower of their respective trades.'[5]

Over the period from the middle of the century until beyond the mid-1880s this remained an accurate characterization of the trade unions in Leeds and, from 1862, of the Leeds Trades Council (LTC), which was a representative federation of the unions in the town. The attitude is clearly expressed in what is probably the earliest collective statement of

the 'new model' trades of Leeds, in the form of an 'Address To the offi-
cers and members of the various Trade Societies of the United Kingdom
and others interested in Trades Unions and Social Science', issued in
1871 from Parkers Temperance Hotel, Briggate. This was a response to
a meeting of the National Association for the Promotion of Social
Science, which had been convened in Leeds, and where one of the speak-
ers had condemned trade-unionism as an unnatural barrier to free trade.

In response, the LTC held a general conference on 2 December 1871
which turned out to be a forum for an indictment of 'that economic
school which classes labour with chattels to be bought, sold, and cheap-
ened in the best markets ...'[6] The conference was a representative one,
chaired by E. C. Denton of the Amalgamated Society of Carpenters
and Joiners (ASCJ) and the first President of the LTC, and attended by
delegates of fifteen of the organized trades of the town. On the platform
was Robert Meek Carter, the Liberal MP for Leeds, and George Potter,
an active member of the co-operative movement. The arguments put
forward at the conference indicate three characteristics of Leeds trade-
unionism in 1871. Firstly, it was an exclusive formation at the top of
the working class; secondly, it had allied itself politically with the radical
wing of the Leeds Liberal Party which, for a number of years, had been
attacking the free-market approach that was characteristic of moderate
liberalism in the town; and thirdly, it was regarded as an essential mech-
anism with which to foster a co-operative and productive relationship
between capital and labour. The aggressive functions of trade unions were
acknowledged (of which strikes were, principally, the essence) and
were justified *in extremis* in order to balance the power of organized
labour against the dominant power of capital. Above all, however, trade
unions were presented as collective self-help organizations providing
otherwise unavailable benefits. Many delegates testified that the average
minimum wage claimed in many trades was a means of protecting not
the labouring classes generally but the interests of skilled workers. The
evidence of George Potter is particularly interesting on this point:

> The rule was to fix an average wage according to the fair value of
> the labour of the majority of the men, and it was the object of the
> unions to legislate not for the inferior men but for the average skilled
> workmen. With the society with which he was connected the rule of
> admission was that the man should be proposed and seconded by men
> who had worked with him, and who could testify that he was at least
> an average man. If he was not an average man he was not admitted,
> because the society was intended for skilled workmen – for men who
> could give a fair equivalent in labour for a fair wage. (Hear, hear)[7]

The trade unions which made up the LTC were of two kinds. Some,
like the Leeds and District Willeyers' and Fettlers' Union, were purely

local unions; others – by 1870 probably a majority – were local branches of the national amalgamated societies. Their rule books suggest the degree of discipline exercised by the union over its membership, as well as the control within the trade that the establishment of such a discipline could secure. It was, for example, both expensive and difficult to become a member of the Willeyers' and Fettlers' Union. Anyone wishing to join had to be proposed by two existing members who could certify that the applicant had at least two years' experience of the trade and was competent in all its branches. His entry was also dependent upon the good state of health, not only of himself, but also of his wife. Perhaps the biggest obstacle of all was that the entrance fee for joining the union was as high as 10*s*. (50p) for men aged over forty years, with a fortnightly contribution of 1*s*.3*d*. (6p). The union exercised a close regulation over the conduct of the membership. It was obligatory for members to take office in the union if elected. Drunkenness, neglect, or disorderly conduct, if they led to dismissal, disqualified the member from eligibility for out-of-work benefit. The control exercised by the union over the conduct of the membership on strike was even more formidable. All members on strike or unemployed at their own trade had to take temporary employment outside that trade if offered, and to pay a proportion of the pay into the society's funds. The committee of the union had the power to compel any member receiving strike pay to take a situation in any town.

The high benefits and contributions and the close supervision of membership activity during a strike were, of course, designed to improve the bargaining position of the union in the labour market and particularly to lessen the opportunity for undercutting the minimum rates in the trade, but the overall objective fell neatly in line with the attitudes expressed during the Trades Conference of 1871. The purpose of union activity was to elevate the economic, moral and intellectual standing of the membership and not to exercise class or trade aggression for its own sake. Rule 62 made this clear: 'Any member boasting of his independence towards his employer, because of his connection with this society shall, on the same being proved, be fined 2*s*. 6*d*. [12½p].'

Unfortunately, not many records of the trade unions of Leeds have survived. Those that do, before the period of new unionism, carry the same kind of sentiments and objectives expressed by the Leeds willeyers and fettlers. The trade unions which came into existence over the period 1850–70 generally regarded themselves as provident societies, as regulators of wages and conditions, and as having a beneficial impact for society generally. The evidence presented to the Royal Commission on the Organisation and Rules of Trades Unions (1867) by the trade-union representatives stressed that codes of procedure between employers and workmen had been established in many trades and that this had a stabilizing influence on industrial relations.

Skilled men organized in unions provided the best protection against strikes because, in the words of the Amalgamated Society of Silk Twisters (established 1866): 'Non-unionists are undoubtedly the most dangerous men in the trade; they are generally the first cause of a strike and would, if permitted, impose upon the society's funds ... they are the most illiterate and least skilled of the men, and generally addicted to intemperance.'[8] The evidence quoted here has been taken from trade-union sources, the intention being to present a description of the self-image of trade-unionists in the period, characterized by Sidney and Beatrice Webb as the period of the new spirit and the new model.[9]

But if supporters of trade unions argued that they were a stable and moderating influence in society, many employers argued that their influence was destructive and their powers too great. Such views were strongly held by some employers of labour in Leeds, particularly in the building industry. James Wilson appeared before the 1867 Royal Commission as a representative of the Leeds Branch of the General Builders' Association. He gave evidence of two kinds. Firstly, he presented a graphic account of what appears to have been the stranglehold established on the conditions of trade by the Leeds branch of the Operative Plasterers' Association (OPA). Secondly, he communicated a statement issued by a meeting of employers in Leeds on 3 April 1867, chaired by Andrew Fairbairn, one of the largest employers of engineering workers in the town. Wilson's evidence about the influence of the trade union in his own trade is thus supplemented by a wider range of opinion amongst employers in Leeds. The OPA charged an entrance fee of 22s.6d. (£1.12½), and men who did not or could not pay the fee (a high one, amounting to three-quarters of a full week's wage) were driven out of employment. The union was financially very strong, non-union shops were boycotted, the men were intimidated, and if non-union workers were approached by employers they found themselves persuaded by the union to withdraw their labour with the promise that their wages would be paid until they could find work in society shops. In the 1860s the union was successful in forcing a wage increase of 6s. (30p) per week; in reducing working hours; in imposing an apprenticeship limitation of three per employer; and in controlling the work rate so that jobs were slowed down to the pace of the less skilled workmen. The relationship between employer and employee was fundamentally altered by the establishment of the union.

Employers responded by issuing a declaration in favour of free trade in labour, in which they proclaimed an attitude that was to be of key importance in its influence on the wider political question of the relationships between organized labour and Liberal politics:

Trades unions. In discussing the action and results of trades unions, the employers desire to recognize and adopt the following principles:

1.   'Free trade in labour'. Every workman has the right to sell, and every employer to purchase his labour on such terms as they mutually agree upon. Labour should form no exception to the law of free trade, which is sufficient to regulate the price of all other commodities.

2nd.   The high or low rate of wages depends not upon the price of provisions, but on the demand, and supply of labour ...

3rd.   That all combinations, whether of workmen to force up or employers to keep down the price of labour, are injurious, and should cease ... If these principles be correct and were carried out, then it follows that every workman would be at liberty. 1st, To work without joining any combination or union. 2nd, To work any number of hours which he desires or necessities led him to undertake. 3rd, To work at any kind of employment ... which was at the time in greatest demand, although differing from his own particular branch of trade. 4th, To work piece or contract work, and by so doing increase, in proportion to his skill and industry his weekly earnings ... The result of all this would be. 6th, That each workman would find his own level.

The working of trades unions has brought about results the reverse of the above, for by their rules neither employer nor workmen can be free agents ...[10]

Not all employers in Leeds took this view and those who had a wider view of the problems of politics and society were able to take, as the 1860s gave way to the 1870s, a more enlightened and tolerant view of trade unions than the attitude expressed in the Leeds declaration quoted above. These new model employers, as Harrison calls them[11] – usually men of large and well-established businesses – believed in the wisdom of high wages and favoured the legal recognition of trade unions, which, to a large degree, was achieved by the late 1870s. Yet, if some employers held this positive view of trade-unionism, there are clear indications that there were many others in Leeds, many of them Liberals, who did not. In the nineteenth century Leeds was predominantly Liberal in its politics. With the role of the working-class electorate becoming increasingly important after the Reform Acts of 1867 and 1884, the relationship of the trades, the labour movement, and the working class generally was to become, for Liberals, a problem of crucial importance to the future shape of political power in the town.

The labour movement: co-operatives

The co-operative movement in the period between 1850 and 1880 was at least as important, and, in the minds of some, more important than trade-unionism as a grouping within the labour movement. Co-operation nationally had undergone a critical transition in the middle of the century, from community building to shopkeeping, as Pollard described it,[12] and the transition was clearly marked in Leeds. The changes have been well described by Harrison.[13]

Leeds socialists, like John Francis Bray in the 1830s, regarded co-operation primarily as a system of social justice founded on the claim that the worker should own in full the product of his labour. However, by the middle years of the century, co-operation in Leeds had developed along a different path. Collectively and individually, those who favoured co-operation came to share something of the interests and responsibilities of those who accumulated capital. In 1854 Lloyd Jones (an Owenite and Christian Socialist and an exponent of co-operative organization) attempted to form a new society in Leeds in which the profits would be used for the further development of co-operative principles, in manufacturing workshops as well as retail stores, the ultimate objective being the formation of a self-governing co-operative community. The proposal failed to get sufficient subscribers – 'the Queenswood cloud hung over Leeds, and distrust checked every proposal of social reformers'[14] – and from 1865 the movement in Leeds moved firmly in the direction of consumers' co-operation. The Leeds District Flour Mill Society, established in 1847, developed later into the Leeds Industrial Co-operative Society (LICS). Retail trading expanded successfully and, instead of using this success as a springboard into co-operative factories, land was purchased in 1871 for new stores at Hunslet, Bramley, Burmantofts and Meanwood. Although an educational fund was established in 1872, resistance to any additional expenditure which might diminish the dividend was strong: 'We want no eddication [sic], give us a bonus' was the call of one meeting.

Given the potentially revolutionary character of the ideas involved in the inception of the co-operative movement in the 1830s and 1840s, the contrast is striking. Co-operation no longer spoke for a whole class, but for the prudent portion of it. Education no longer served to illuminate the progress of the proletariat as a class, but to improve the opportunity for individual advancement. Summing up the social achievement of co-operation in Leeds G. J. Holyoake inadvertently emphasized the change over the period between 1840 and 1880: 'Co-operation at least has had this merit – it has taught workmen of the roughest class to behave like gentlemen.'[15]

The labour movement and Liberal politics

The Liberals dominated local politics in Leeds for 60 years from 1835, except for occasional Conservative upsurges. In the first election of the reformed council the Liberals took 42 out of the 48 seats. Conservatives came close to gaining control only in 1841 and 1874, but in neither year did the full challenge materialize, and in 1880 the Liberals controlled the council by 53 to 11.[16] In parliamentary politics also Liberals domi-nated Leeds by almost the same margin as they had done in local elections. Yet these results disguise a polling situation that was in fact much more evenly balanced, with the Conservatives consistently achieving between 35 per cent and 50 per cent of the poll. The Liberals were therefore faced in Leeds with a persistent Conservative challenge. Much of the Liberal domination of Leeds politics from mid-century up until 1895 can be explained by the support, particularly after 1867, of a dominant part of organized labour in the town. This alignment had its origins polit-ically in the decline of militant Chartism and Owenite socialism, and economically in the consolidation of self-help values and organizations.

Leeds Liberals, or the more far-sighted of them, had promoted early attempts at class conciliation. The formation of the Leeds Parliamentary Reform Association in 1840 by Hamer Stansfield, J. G. Marshall and Samuel Smiles, which led middle-class radicalism towards the support of household suffrage, was a recognition that 'without working class support there seemed little hope of securing those reforms which were necessary to complete the economic and social hegemony of the middle classes'.[17] By 1855 the Leeds Chartists had formed the Leeds Advanced Liberal Party, and when the Leeds Working Men's Parliamentary Reform Association was established in 1860, led by men who had previously been Chartists, the gathering strength of a conciliatory mood was clear. The Yorkshire Reform Conference of 1861 showed the new attitudes of the respectable working man confidently displayed. The conference was to be the occasion of a movement being set on foot 'such as would combine together all the intelligent working men of the country'. The real business of the conference lay in deciding at what point the line should be drawn. For Edward Baines (proprietor of the Leeds Mercury) a measure was required which would include only 'the better and edu-cated part of the working classes', a position attacked by the Liberal MP for Leeds, Robert Meek Carter, who believed that such 'milk and water' proposals would make the people apathetic and indifferent. The workers suspected that the middle class did not propose to confer the franchise on them, and, indeed, Baines' Bill (a proposal for a more limited exten-sion of the franchise than that finally adopted in 1867) would give the vote to shopkeepers, clerks, bookkeepers, and 'the higher grades of mech-anics, but not to the bulk of the working classes'.[18] For Baines, the fact that his Bill would add 4,500 names to the electorate was sufficient.

The debate at the 1861 Leeds conference, and its outcome, was of basic importance to the future social alignment that was to make up Leeds liberalism. The moderate Liberals, represented by Baines and Marshall, felt that their politics would benefit from a line drawn between the skilled and unskilled working class. Radical Liberals, represented by Carter and F. Spark, proprietor of the *Leeds Express*, had a far broader and more generous conception of liberalism, encompassing a view of politics which was based on a belief that bridges needed to be built between the industrial middle class and the working-class community. They realized that the future of liberalism depended on the continued development of working-class organizations in such a way as to link their interests with liberalism in the area of industry as much as in the arena of politics. Indeed, much of the future of the Leeds Liberal Party, in its relationship to the labour movement, hinged on the outcome of the clash between radical Carterite liberalism on the one hand and traditional liberalism on the other.

Moderate liberalism was represented by the *Leeds Mercury*, the direct mouthpiece of the Baines family until 1870, when T. W. Reid was made editor. Reid himself then continued to expound what he considered to be Bainesite politics. Baines' proposal for a limited household suffrage was opposed in Leeds by Carter and the *Leeds Express*[19] and was swept aside by the Reform League agitation. As a consequence, his measure was superseded by a much more inclusive one, which, it was estimated, increased the electoral register from 8,000 to 30,000. In this new era the *Mercury* and moderate liberalism hoped that organized labour would be a docile and willing ally. Its attitude to the economic problems of labour was generally hostile and conventionally fixed within the free-market notions of buying and selling labour. With unemployment figures rising towards the end of the 1870s, and as the severe depression increasingly hit Leeds industries, even the skilled trade unions began to feel threatened. However, the *Mercury* regarded the depression to be, in part, a consequence of the activities of trade-unionism, and in the 1870s and 1880s the newspaper constantly attacked the futility of industrial militancy. The economic problems of society, it argued, stemmed not from structural causes but from the moral weakness of individuals, and the consequent remedy was thrift and sobriety.[20]

On the other hand, the radicalism of the *Leeds Express*, and particularly of Carter, displayed a more sympathetic insight in relation to the economic problems of working people, and of the connection between labour politics and liberalism. Robert Meek Carter (1814–82) was typical of the group of largely self-made small businessmen who came to play a prominent part in Leeds politics in the third quarter of the nineteenth century. He was born in Skeffing in the East Riding and worked as a farm labourer, until, at the age of 16, he moved to Leeds to find employment in a gig mill. After attending night school at Marshall's Library in

Wortley Lane he rose to the position of foreman, changed his trade in 1844 when he became a coal weighman, and shortly afterwards set up business as a coal merchant. He entered politics in 1850, when he was returned unopposed as a radical for Holbeck Ward, and began a twenty-five year period of involvement with working-class political activities. He was made an alderman in 1862, was a Liberal MP for Leeds between 1868 and 1876, and from 1862 was a leading figure in the Leeds Co-operative Society, the Mechanics' Institute, the Leeds Working Men's Association (LWMA), and the Leeds Manhood Suffrage Association.[21] Along with men like James Hole, Lloyd Jones and Edwin Gaunt,[22] Carter's influence on the shaping of a radical approach towards the 'labour problem' was an important one. The *Leeds Express*, founded in 1857, came under the control of Carter and F. R. Spark shortly afterwards. Carter, following his central role in the formation of the LWMA in the early 1860s, had close links with the organized working class in Leeds, and the *Express* rapidly developed a clear commitment towards the representation of working-class interests. The attitude which the *Express* took to labour questions throughout the late 1860s and the 1870s was based on a view of politics outlined in a series of articles which ran under the heading "The Labour and Capital Question". Written by 'A Co-operator' they represented the combined view of Carter, Spark and other radicals who realized that bold solutions had to be found for the 'labour problem'. The approach was based on four premises: that the gulf between employers and employed was widening socially and economically; that the moral improvement of the working classes depended first of all upon their material improvement; that civilized social relationships would eventually disintegrate, since 'poverty and barbarism are co-related and inseparable'; and that, consequently, a new art of government was required.[23]

This radical Liberal position went alongside a broader view which saw society divided essentially not between labour and capital but between the productive and the unproductive; between those involved in industrial activity generating wealth and those living off unearned income, primarily landed wealth. The political goal for liberalism was, therefore, to unite the interests of the industrial classes – employer and worker – and to consolidate and advance those interests against a wasteful aristocracy and the social groups which shared its values.

By the 1880s, organized labour at least, if not the broader working class, was generally considered to be Liberal in electoral loyalty and one of the cornerstones of Liberal electoral power. Carter and the *Leeds Express* realized that this allegiance could never be taken for granted, and a view of politics for labour was advocated which depended on the extension of providential self-help institutions throughout the whole of the working class. Sound trade unions would lead to the development of conciliation machinery. The promotion of attitudes of class harmony

through co-operative enterprise would result in the emergence of industrial co-partnership between employers and workers, while legislative
action in Parliament would be enacted to humanize the factory. All this
would take place within an overall ideology of co-operation between the
harmonious interests of all those in the productive (industrial) sector of
society, politically united against parasitic aristocratic and landed interests.
This attractive view of politics, which had a sense both of economic and
political democracy, presented the best hope for the Liberal Party if
it was to continue to build on the electoral allegiance of labour in the
decades of the 1880s and 1890s. It is worth noting that Leeds was a
centre in which the quest for democracy – for a liberty tree which was
nourished politically and economically – was vigorously pursued. In the
following chapters we shall see how this quest was to fare.

Notes

1. E. P. Thompson, *The Making of the English Working Class* (London, 1968);
    J. F. C. Harrison 'Chartism in Leeds', in A. Briggs (ed.), *Chartist Studies*
    (London, 1963).
2. For a full account of the national electoral politics of this period see
    H. J. Hanham, *Elections and Party Management* (London, 1959).
3. Reform League, *Report on Leeds* (George Howell Collection, Bishopsgate
    Institute, London, 1868).
4. These figures are calculated from data in G. Rimmer, 'Occupations in Leeds
    1841–1951', *Thoresby Society Miscellany* 14, 2 (1967), pp. 158–78; and in
    S. and B. Webb, *History of Trade Unionism* (London, 1911), p. 414.
5. Statistical Tables and Report on Trade Unions 1887, PP (1887), LXXXIX.
6. Leeds and District Trades Council, Conference of Trades Delegates (Leeds,
    1871).
7. *Ibid.*, p. 9.
8. *Royal Commission on the Organisation and Rules of Trade Unions* (1867), PP
    1868–1869, XXXI, p. 459.
9. Webb, *History of Trade Unionism*, Chapters IV and V.
10. *Royal Commission*, pp. 232–3, Q. 4572.
11. R. Harrison, *Before The Socialists* (London, 1965), p. 37.
12. S. Pollard, 'Nineteenth Century Co-operation: From Community Build-
    ing to Shopkeeping', in A. Briggs and J. Saville (eds.), *Essays in Labour History*
    (London, 1967), pp. 74–113.
13. J. F. C. Harrison, *Learning and Living 1790–1960* (London, 1961); also his
    'Chartism in Leeds', and *Social Reform in Victorian Leeds: The Work of James
    Hole 1820–1895* (1954).
14. G. J. Holyoake, *Jubilee History of the Leeds Industrial Co-operative Society*
    (Manchester, 1897), p. 53. This was a reference to the failure of one of the
    largest of the co-operative communities set up by Robert Owen.
15. The above quotes are from Holyoake, *The Leeds Industrial Co-operative
    Society*.

16. D. Fraser, 'Areas of Urban Politics, Leeds 1830–1880', in H. Dyos and M. Wolff (eds.), *The Victorian City* II (London, 1973), p. 779.
17. Harrison, 'Chartism in Leeds', p. 85.
18. *Report of the Proceedings of the Yorkshire Reform Conference* (Leeds, 1861).
19. This account of the politics of the Leeds Liberal Press is derived largely from D. Jones, 'The Liberal Press and The Rise of Labour: A Study with particular reference to Leeds and Bradford, 1850–1895', Ph.D. thesis (University of Leeds, 1973); for details of the formation of the *Leeds Express*, see p. 66.
20. Jones, 'The Liberal Press', pp. 114–15.
21. This profile of Carter is based on the obituary in the *Leeds Express*, 9 August 1882; Holyoake, *The Leeds Industrial Co-operative Society*, p. 249; Harrison, *Social Reform in Victorian Leeds*, p. 57.
22. For biographies of Hole, Jones, Gaunt and Bell, see Harrison, *Social Reform in Victorian Leeds*, pp. 57–8.
23. *Leeds Express*, 5 November 1884: 'The Labour and Capital Question No. 2'.

Chapter 2

The Liberal Party and the Labour Movement, 1880–1890

There are questions, however, coming up in leaps and bounds that will even brush aside for a time the liquor questions ... I mean social- ism ... For over five years I have been warning friends that unless the Liberal Party took up and considered these questions and dealt with them, a great Labour Party would spring up and sweep aside both Tories and Liberals as such and govern for themselves. You may think this utopian; it remains so until the hour, and not a moment beyond, when the masses have accumulated funds to sustain their men for their cause. Whether Liberals take up these questions or not is for them to decide.

J. S. Mathers, Liberal Party election agent, November 1895.[1]

Liberal–Labour politics in the 1880s

It has been argued in the previous chapter that one of the major reasons for the dominance of the Liberal Party in Leeds was due to the loyalty of an influential part of the organized labour movement. A. Roberts has shown that the party was successful also because it represented the Non- conformist and temperance interest generally.[2] The progressive Liberals had won the broad sympathy of the organized labour movement because of the positive role they had played in the parliamentary reform cam- paigns of the 1860s. In addition, they had developed a concept of political action based on the promotion of the interests of working-class orga- nizations. The challenge for the Leeds Liberal Party in the 1880s was to apply this concept of a positive role for the labour movement as a legit- imate interest group within their own political framework.

The signs were favourable in 1880 for the continuation of good Liberal–Labour relations. The control of the Leeds Liberal Association over Liberal politics in the town was firmly established by 1880 in the hands of James Kitson, the engineer, J. S. Mathers, a building-society manager, and T. W. Reid, editor of the *Leeds Mercury* – all Liberal

26

moderates – and the Trades Council seemed, on the whole, content to acquiesce in this arrangement. Attempts to secure the independent political organization of labour had not met with much success in the years up until 1880, and in Leeds the branch of the Labour Representation League was absorbed as the radical wing of the local Liberal Association.[3] The Leeds Trades Council in 1882, the year from which its minute books are preserved, had not changed significantly from that which had existed in the late 1860s and early 1870s. Up until 1885 there were only two trades councils in Yorkshire – in Leeds (formed in 1860) and in Bradford (formed in 1868). Trades councils were later formed in Huddersfield (1885), Halifax (1889), Keighley (1890) and Wakefield (1891), but those in Leeds and Bradford were by far the biggest with membership figures above 10,000 by the 1890s.[4] In 1868 the Leeds labour movement was composed of 27 organized trade societies. In July 1882 the LTC represented 32 trade societies, indicating a very slow rate of increase over the period.[5]

These figures can only be taken as approximately correct since union statistics were not collected by the Labour Department of the Board of Trade until the 1890s. Trade-union strength in the early 1880s must, therefore, in the main be gauged from local observations and from the rather patchy account which emerges from the records of the LTC. At the opening of the 1880s organized labour in Leeds still overwhelmingly represented the élite of skilled trade-unionists, many of whose leaders had Liberal Party affiliations. Henry Maundrill (miner), William Bune (brushmaker), William Marston (tailor), John Judge (boot and shoe operative), and Owen Connellan (typographer-printer) were all members of the Liberal Party in Leeds, and the last three in particular, were to be the dominant personalities directing the affairs of the LTC in the 1880s and through the 1890s. Judge, it is true, took a more radical position than the others, since, although he was a strong advocate of labour representation within a radical Liberal Party framework if possible, he was prepared to become independent of the party if not. Nevertheless, he was staunchly opposed to socialists gaining political control of the movement and led the fight against them during the period when new unions of the semi-skilled and unskilled, led by socialists, emerged around 1889–90.

The Trades Council was a firm supporter of free trade and its view of the causes of the economic problems of society did not stray far from the explanations conventionally offered by the Liberal Party. The most significant cause was said to be 'the present land system, in diverting the labourers into the towns' and consequently overstocking the labour market. This perception played a significant part in the electoral approach of the Liberal Party in Leeds in the attempt to attract the labour vote. The debates in the Trades Council in the early and mid-1880s were often provoked by a desire to understand the effects of the depression in trade

and the increasing insecurity that pervaded the labour market, compared
with the relative prosperity of the previous decade. In 1883 it was suggested at a meeting of the LTC that the delegates should support a
scheme to set up emigration clubs to enable working people to go to
Canada and other colonies to find work.[6] And in 1890 it expressed the
unanimous opinion that the government should relieve the congested
labour market and the chronic poverty among the unskilled labourers of
Great Britain 'by the promotion of colonies in which work should be
provided for the unskilled'.[7]

Socialist solutions for the problems of unemployment, and the general complaints of organized labour were firmly rejected. In 1887 Tom
Mann had published his pamphlet 'What a Compulsory Eight Hour
Working Day Means to the Workers', in which he put forward the argument for a legislated eight-hour day, a measure which would, in Mann's
view, reduce unemployment, strengthen working-class organization, and
make possible further political advance. It did not meet with approval on
its initial introduction in Leeds.[8] In December 1887 the question of the
legislated eight-hour day came up for discussion, following the receipt
of a circular on the subject from the parliamentary committee of the TUC.
Henry Maundrill of the local Miners' Federation, secretary of the
LTC and a Liberal Party member, proposed a motion asserting that
the LTC disapproved of Parliament's interference in the regulation of the
hours of labour, and received unanimous support.[9]

But the interests of labour were not always so close to Liberal politics.
The realities of the workplace could starkly contradict the ideal liberal
principle of a harmony of interest between classes in industrial society.
On the one hand, there was an underlying hostility to trade-unionism
amongst politically influential employers in Leeds. For its part, the normally genial and courteous LTC could become aggressively alert when
trade-union rights were challenged, and it defended them vehemently.

There are clear indications in the 1880s that skilled trade-unionists
were increasingly threatened by the introduction of new technologies
and the extension of the subdivision of labour. Complaints about dilu-
tion and de-skilling began to appear from the early 1880s. In February
1883, for example, John Judge gave notice to the LTC of a dispute by his
own society – of boot and shoe riveters – caused by a manufacturer in
Leeds attempting to organize a greater subdivision of labour and employing boys to do what had previously been men's work. Again, in November
of that year, a deputation of engineers from Fowlers of Hunslet com-
plained to the LTC about the replacement of skilled by unskilled labour
and a consequent imposed reduction in wages.[10] Under this pressure,
the LTC and the skilled trades that it represented found themselves
occasionally forced to adopt aggressive postures, and to take up positions which supported the whole of the working-class interest.

This broader class interest was exhibited in many ways. For example, throughout the 1880s the LTC pursued the interests of workers who made claims under the Employers' Liability Act. These cases may seem parochial, but they occasionally gained great symbolic value. In May 1883, for example, a Mrs Mitchell made a claim following the death of her husband at Messrs Holdsworths, Leeds engineers. The verdict in the County Court went in favour of the claimant, but the insurance agents appealed on behalf of the company. The LTC immediately launched a minor crusade in the town: meetings were held at Vicar's Croft and on Hunslet and Holbeck Moors; a bellman was employed to walk through Hunslet to give details of the case; and £93 was collected in public donations. When the insurance company lost its appeal, large crowds led by brass bands took to the streets in the working-class areas of Hunslet and Holbeck to display their delight.[11] This display was indicative of the community of interest which could emerge amongst the workforce in the town, and indicated the underlying potential for a communal base to deal with conflicts between employers and employees. In September and October 1884 the LTC welcomed the delegates of the newly formed Leeds Jewish Tailors' Machinists' Society, and assisted the attempts of weavers' unions in Huddersfield and Batley to recruit amongst the poorly organized weavers in Leeds. In November 1885 the LTC began a campaign to organize the women employed in the tailoring trade. Indeed, the willingness of the skilled trades to help with the organization of the unskilled has perhaps been underestimated. It is true that they would not generally accept the unskilled into their own societies, but the LTC was very active during the strikes of the unskilled, which began in 1889. The builders' labourers and the gas workers, organized by the socialists outside the LTC, were welcomed in October 1889, and in the autumn of 1889 the LTC itself launched into a campaign to organize the men working on the Leeds tramways to reduce their excessively long hours of labour.

Under these kinds of pressure the Liberal's alliance with the Labour movement, never formalized but traditionally effective, was clearly beginning to come under some strain. The adoption of working-class candidates by the Liberal Party had actually declined in 1880 compared with 1874.[12] Leeds had not had an MP with a primary interest in labour questions since the resignation from Parliament of R. M. Carter in 1876, and there are indications that the LTC regretted the diminution of its political influence with the Liberal Party.

Another group of independent radicals, led by the secularist and freethinker Charles Bradlaugh, advocated that working-class radicals should seek political representation irrespective of Liberal Party opinion. John Judge fitted more into the mould of a Bradlaugh radical, and cautiously attempted to move the LTC in that direction. In March 1885 he called a special meeting to discuss labour representation and succeeded in passing the following resolution:

At the first General Election under the Redistribution Bill a bona fide Labour candidate should be brought forward for adoption by one of the divisions of this borough and that we recommend the same to the consideration of the Trades Societies of the town and working men generally.[13]

Such initiatives came to very little. Despite the efforts of Judge, those candidates who were initially approached to represent labour in Leeds at parliamentary level, including Henry Broadhurst of the TUC, declined, and the LTC agreed in the end to wait on the Liberal Association in the Leeds South constituency in the hope that they would favourably consider the claims of labour. By the end of the decade, however, new groups and ideas were entering the organized labour movement in the towns. Unskilled and semi-skilled workers, influenced by socialist ideas, introduced a new urgency into the debate on 'the labour question', as we shall see in the next chapter.

In November 1890 Herbert Gladstone, son of William Ewart Gladstone (Prime Minister 1868–74, 1880–5, 1886 and 1892–4) and Liberal MP for West Leeds, addressed the LTC in a meeting which crystallized the dilemmas for a labour movement which was instinctively Lib–Lab, but which needed to find a new legitimacy to speak for the labour movement as a whole.[14] Both the LTC and the Liberal political leadership in Leeds became aware at the end of the decade that the new unionist strikes of 1889–90 and the revival of interest in socialist ideas potentially threatened the Liberal's relationship with the labour movement. The debate provides little evidence that Herbert Gladstone understood the nature of the labour problem, or that he or the LTC leaders were competent to deal with the larger philosophical questions which had been debated nationally throughout the 1880s in the attempt to update liberalism and to renew its relevance to urban industrial problems. The principle of Liberal legislation, Gladstone argued, was to make labour and capital equal before the law, and to extend the legal rights of working people. This was a traditional if rather narrow and dull conception of liberalism, which failed to catch the mood that was beginning to develop that a concept of community welfare and a positive role for government was needed to supplement individual legal rights. Yet an imaginative and bold approach to questions of social welfare and labour relations was largely absent from Gladstone's priorities.

Radical liberalism in the 1880s

In January 1885 John Judge attended the Industrial Remuneration Conference (IRC), held in the Prince's Hall, London, under the presidency of Sir Charles Dilke.[15] The objective of the conference was to devise a programme which was capable of answering the question posed by Sir Thomas Brassey, the Liberal industrialist, at the opening session: 'Does any man question the advantage of a more equal distribution of wealth, or a closer community of interests between capitalists and workmen?'[16] The conference was part of a series of endeavours which began from the 1880s in the attempt to develop a new liberalism, and which did indeed result in an impressive extension of a socially responsible and ethical liberalism at the level of political theory. The role of the labour movement in this new liberalism was clearly expressed by L. T. Hobhouse. Hobhouse was concerned to find a means of reconciling the attitudes and organizations of labour with the objectives of liberal social theory, and in his work *The Labour Movement* (1893) he stressed the creative role of the leading institutions of organized labour in developing the mutual aid and collective self-help characteristics which he thought to be essential qualities of a truly liberal society. The principle of co-operation and the advantages it brings (the matching of supply and demand and the sharing of profit) may be extended, he argued, to the activities of the municipality and the state:

> Put the municipality in charge of that which is municipal in extent and the nation in control of that which is national. In this way the principle of control by the body of consumers proceeds most easily and speedily by several convergent roads. And on each method the effects are the same. We avoid the waste and friction at present involved in the adjustment of demand and supply; and we put the surplus revenue into the pockets, not of individuals, but of the community. Lastly, we introduce a new spirit and a new principle into industry.[17]

The expansion of trade-unionism and the growth of its association with co-operative enterprise were to provide the means of ensuring that co-operative employees, whether in the retail stores, the municipal enterprises, or in state employment, would be adequately remunerated. Freeden[18] has shown that, from the 1880s, Liberals reformulated their views and definitions on a whole range of issues, such as rights, property, equality of opportunity, the individual in relation to the state, citizenship, communal responsibility and social welfare, without compromising what was inherently liberal in its outlook. This development was made by a relatively small group of political theorists and by a larger group of liberal thinkers with an influence on the press. Through the 1890s and up to 1914 liberalism changed significantly as a body of ideas, stressing social reform and emphasizing the fulfilment of individual needs within the community, while accepting an expanded positive role for the state in social and welfare activities.

A strong underlying suspicion of the state was common to most Liberals, whose deep-seated value of self-help was preferred to state intervention whenever possible. John Judge, attending the IRC from Leeds, will have heard about the detailed justification of schemes to improve and increase the dignity and liberty of labour without having to adopt the drastic theories and measures of socialism. Those who advocated grander solutions, including collectivism and state socialism, were clearly in a minority. Their case, however, was strongly represented. Frederic Harrison (an Oxford graduate, lawyer and radical reformer) argued that the partial collective self-help schemes did little to harmonize capital and labour:

> After all has been allowed for the work done by trade unions, co-operation, benefit societies and the like, it touches only a fortunate few ...
>
> Co-operation, in particular, has a melancholy failure to acknowledge. Too much has been made of the fact that a small fraction of the labouring classes (600,000 or 700,000 all told) have learned to buy their tea and sugar in economical ways at stores and clubs. There is no social millennium in this ...
>
> A powerful trades union often improves the condition of the whole trade. But, at the utmost, trades unions substantially affect only the minority ... In two generations now it has shown itself utterly powerless to reach the residuum, or even materially to combine the great average mass. It tends rather to sectional and class interests; it divides trade from trade, members from non-members; and especially it accentuates that sinister gulf which separates the skilled and well-paid artisans from the unskilled labourer, and from the vast destitute residuum.[19]

However, the mood and spirit of the conference, as summed up by Sir Charles Dilke, was one of class harmony:

> There have been a great many more workmen who have addressed us than capitalists; indeed, the majority of those who have taken part in the proceedings of the three days have been workmen and delegates of workmen's associations of various kinds. But that has not occurred here which would be likely to occur abroad, and which often does occur in foreign countries, that all the workmen take one side, and all the capitalists and other than workmen take the other.[20]

In the quest for common ground, the Labour Association[21] pressed the claims of profit-sharing in industry and the extension of the co-operative model. Co-partnership and co-operation, as ideas of industrial organization, were admirably suited to the object of reconciling labour and capital. Edward Greening, speaking for the newly formed Labour

Co-Partnership Association, pointed out that profit-sharing provided workers with a resource beyond wages which could be capitalized to provide a fund for old age, sickness and death. The advocacy of the co-operative method was seen as serving an ideological function, while at the same time resting on sound commercial principles.

The co-operative movement

While labour movement radicals in Leeds did, on occasion, justify the interference of the state in the regulation of industrial conditions (as with the factory inspectorate) on the whole they opposed the extension of the functions of the centralized state. Before 1890 and the raising of the socialist debate, it was felt that justice for labour could best be attained by voluntarist self-help. The philosophy of the transformation of competitive individual capitalism into a kind of federated co-operative competition, without the need for the expansion of central state functions, had strong potential bases of support within the labour movement nationally and locally from the early 1880s. It would seem, at first sight, that in the 1880s the Leeds labour movement could well have developed in the way that leading liberal theorists prescribed. The co-operative movement was strong; as Beatrice Webb (née Potter) remarked in 1891: '... Leeds, Oldham, and Newcastle are strongholds in the very heart of the Co-operative State'.[22]

Although the co-operative movement was concentrated primarily in the business of retail trade, the Co-operative Wholesale Society, trading from 1864 and with a branch in Leeds from 1882, employed 4,600 people in manufacturing occupations.[23] Nationally, trading co-operatives grew rapidly in the 1870s and 1880s, and Leeds in particular shared in the growth, as shown in Tables 2 and 3.

However, labour politics did not develop in Leeds in the 1880s in the way prescribed by the Liberal radicals, by the delegates to the IRC, and later by Hobhouse. A symbiotic relationship between trade-unionism and co-operation did not develop, and the coherent ideology of a labour movement expanding according to liberal self-help social forms, based on raising workers to the status of labouring capitalists, was not realized in practice. The putative new liberal theory of labour relations was in fact an inadequate one, since it ignored the reality of a severe division in the labour movement itself. What was purported to be a design for action for the labour movement was in fact applicable only to a small proportion of the skilled trades. Co-operation could not provide an acceptable model to guarantee the economic and social security of the unskilled; neither, it became apparent as the 1880s wore on, could it offer a model for reconciling the interests of capital and labour.

Table 2   Co-operative societies in England and Wales: membership and trading statistics

Ten years ending	Established number of societies in existence	Membership	Share capital £	Net profits £
1870	901	248,108	2,035,626	3,212,094
1880	1,015	526,686	5,806,545	12,761,673
1890	1,430	955,393	11,380,210	24,326,790

Source: Royal Commission on Labour (1893–4), PP, XXXIX, Pt. 1, p. 8.

Table 3   Growth of the Leeds Industrial Co-operative Society, 1873–1887

	Membership	Share capital £	Turnover £	Profits £	Branches
1873	9,071	49,649	182,474	14,778	11
1887	20,895	217,940	498,578	55,832	85*

*Plus manufacturing activities in the production of boots and shoes and brush-making.

Sources: Holyoake, *Jubilee History of the Leeds Industrial Co-operative Society* (Manchester, 1897); Royal Commission on Labour (1893–4), PP, XXXIX, Pt. 1.

By 1890 the co-operative movement had lost all interest in debates about the labour theory of value or in altering the balance of power between employer and employee, management and worker. This was clear in the evidence presented by the Co-operative Union to the 1892 Royal Commission on Labour. Speaking for the whole of the English co-operative movement, the Union stressed that while it still felt that its function was to redistribute wealth in favour of the workforce, this was to be achieved by concentrating on the worker as consumer, and not as producer. The advantage of co-operation to its employees was that trade-union rates were paid, and there was less fluctuation in wages because of greater continuity of work.[24]

Profit-sharing with the workforce was also opposed by the Co-operative Wholesale Society, as was worker participation at the level of board of directors. The limitations of the system were pointed out in a series of questions put to J. T. W. Mitchell, the representative of the Co-operative Union and the Co-operative Wholesale Society, by Gerald Balfour, MP:

291. You say that one of the objects of the Co-operative Union is to conciliate the conflicting interests of the capitalist, the workman, and the purchaser, by means of an equitable division among them of profits?
– Yes.

292. I fail as yet to understand in what way your system can affect the relations of capitalist and workman?
– We do it so that the worker gets his share of our profits by being a member of the store and getting it in consumption.

293. That is to say, not in his capacity as worker?
– Not as a workman, but as a worker, so far as he consumes …

294. So far as I can see you are in the position of any joint stock company in your relation to the workers?
– I do not know what you mean by a joint stock company.

295. Or for that matter in the position of any private employer?
– In the position of any private employer in that sense.[25]

Mitchell envisaged that the co-operative societies should grow so that eventually all the retailing business of the country would be carried out on co-operative lines, with every member of the population becoming a member of a co-operative society. In Leeds the success of the Leeds Industrial Co-operative Society (LICS) in the 1880s and 1890s was measured entirely by the annual growth in profit and dividend. A motion to pay the same bonus on wages as on members' purchases was defeated. In a narrowing of perspective which lost sight of the ideas of economic democracy, the directors failed to realize the gap that existed between their activities as co-operators in the 1890s and the objectives for the co-operative movement set by the Rochdale Pioneers (the founders of the modern co-operative movement), when a progression from storekeeping to co-operative factories and ultimately co-operative communities was envisaged. The LICS was embarrassed in the 1880s and 1890s by a surplus of profit (as a result of which it cut the amount of share capital an individual could hold) and put its money into land acquisition, as a secure form of investment, and as a means of extending stores. The Education Department, on the other hand, had a constant struggle to get funds.[26]

Throughout the 50 years of its existence up to 1895 the co-operative movement had been a major agency of liberalization within the community, a dominant institution by which self-made men were enabled to rise.[27] Temperance, self-improvement and co-operation were cardinal virtues uniting all the leaders of the LICS: thus, a Mr. Hunt, elected onto the board of the society in 1849, 'had just married and, like a prudent husband, or probably having a prudent wife, his thoughts were turned to co-operation as a means of improved income'.[28] But as a political force the movement achieved little to answer the charge, increasingly made by socialists, that capital exercised some sort of tyranny over labour.

Labour and electoral politics

Politically, the Liberal Party had strong bases of traditional support in the predominantly working-class areas south of the River Aire. Here, the Liberal strongholds at local level were Bramley Ward, Armley and Wortley, New Wortley, Holbeck, West Hunslet, East Hunslet. North of the river, the Liberals could expect to do well in East, North East and West Wards.

Table 4   Results in parliamentary elections in Leeds, 1885–1895

Constituency	1885	1886	1892	1895
West	L	L	L	L
East	C	L	L	L
North	C	C	C	C
South	L	L	L	L
Central	C	C	C	C

L = Liberal victory.   C = Conservative victory.

At parliamentary level, too, the Liberals were strong in West and South constituencies; that is, precisely in those areas which were composed of the working-class wards south of the river (see Table 4). South Leeds, with an electorate in 1895 of nearly 11,000 from a population of 60,000, was made up of South Ward, East and West Hunslet and part of Bramley Wards, whose population were 'mostly working class employed in the large engineering establishments'.[29]

The *Leeds Mercury* said that the artisan class largely predominated amongst the 12,000 strong electorate of West Leeds, the constituency chosen by Herbert Gladstone on the advice of the moderate Liberal, James Kitson:

> South and West, which are South of the River, are both working class constituencies ... of the two, the West, which includes Holbeck (where is the Co-operators Society and Mill, and many evidences of solid institutions) ... is the one I should take ... I am a member of the 200 of the West, my works are in the division ...[30]

East Leeds was less predictable for the Liberal Party. Although the population of c.60,000 was almost exclusively working class – labourers, colliers, mill-hands, railwaymen and small shopkeepers – the constituency was regarded by the *Leeds Mercury* as a dark horse, partly because the people tended to be from the less skilled working class, 'more susceptible to the publican interests and thus to Toryism'. In 1885 the Irish vote amounted to 2,000, and because this was well organized, the constituency tended to reflect the demands of Irish nationalist politics. The North East ward, in particular, was a stronghold of Irish and publican interests between 1882 and 1885, returning three Tory councillors all of whom were connected with the brewing trade.[31] North Leeds, with a population of 58,000 and an electorate of 10,000 in 1885, contained 'within its borders all the best residential districts in the city, the big houses of the wealthy at Roundhay, Chapeltown, and Headingley, and the villas of those who earn "salaries" instead of "wages"'.[32] There was, however, a growing working-class population in the district of Woodhouse, Burley and Kirkstall as the northward and westward drift of the population increased in the years after 1885.

The creation of new constituencies in 1885 presented further problems for Liberals. Until the general election of 1880, Leeds had returned three members to Parliament. From 1885 it returned five, one from each of five new single-member constituencies (North, East, West, South and Central). It had been felt by Leeds Liberals that the division of the town into five separate constituencies would weaken them because the advantage of an overall Liberal sentiment in the town would be lessened by the creation of a Conservative-orientated middle class, or 'aristocratic' areas, particularly if the river was used as a boundary to divide off suburban from working-class Leeds. In the event the Boundary Commissioners went for a scheme which followed the Conservative Party proposals, using the River Aire as a natural boundary.

Labour and social questions were not ignored in political debate in Leeds between 1885 and 1895, but neither were they seen as leading issues for elections. The question of social reform was a confusing one for Liberals in Leeds, and generally they addressed it only when a Tory opponent accused them of neglecting it. In the 1885 general election campaign the Liberal, Sir Lyon Playfair, pledged that he would 'devote himself to those great social questions in which working men were particularly interested, such as education, public health, thrift, and independence'.[33] Thomas Leuty, fighting North Leeds in 1892, was the most progressive Liberal candidate to emerge in this period; he came out firmly in support of an Eight Hours Bill for miners, and at the by-election for East Leeds in 1895 he argued unambiguously that: 'there was no doubt that the chief future work of the Liberal Party was to deal with social questions ... the condition of the poor ... the problem of those out of work ... and the question of old age pensions.'[34] More typically, such issues were placed behind the traditional Liberal concerns of temperance, educational reform, church disestablishment and, above all, from 1886, Irish Home Rule. In 1886 Leeds Liberals had declared their support for W. E. Gladstone who regarded the Irish problem as the primary political concern of the day. Six years later the question of Irish Home Rule again dominated the Liberal approach to the general election as a means of securing justice for Ireland, and in order to clear the way for domestic reforms, principally based on the Newcastle programme. The general election of 1895 saw labour problems coming into sharper focus because of the background of economic recession against which it took place and because of the presence for the first time of Independent Labour Party (ILP) candidates. The Liberal administration of 1892–95 had disappointed those who had hoped for some progress on social and labour questions. For the first time, dissatisfaction with the Liberal emphasis was publicly voiced by a section of organized labour. During the 1892 general election campaign, despite the municipal strike of 1890 and the emergence of socialism amongst the new unionists, the Liberals Judge, Marston, Bune and Maundrill, and the Lib–Labs, remained in control of the LTC and a policy of general support for the Liberal Party was maintained. By 1895 that support was being increasingly questioned. On 21 April 1895 the ILP held a meeting to consider the possibility of running a candidate in opposition to the Liberal candidate, Leuty, in the by-election for East Leeds, held immediately before the general election. There was obviously a deep division in the LTC; while the ILP was eager to fight, '... others are of the opinion that the Gladstonian candidate's address is "socialistic" or "independent" enough even for the ILP ...'[35]

Although the ILP decided not to run a candidate in the East Leeds by-election this was the beginning of a concerted attempt on behalf of the labour movement to go beyond the traditional issues of Leeds Liberal politics. The North East Ward ILP and the Leeds ILP Central Council condemned both the Liberal and Conservative Parties because 'questions directly affecting the conditions of the working class are relegated to a secondary place and no definite pledges are offered', particularly on the question of proposals for alleviating unemployment.[36] Unperturbed, Leuty went ahead and campaigned on Home Rule and

House of Lords reform; in the event, it was generally felt that the Irish vote won the seat for the Liberals.[37]

In the general election proper of 1895, the first ILP candidate went to the poll: Arthur Shaw, president of the LTC, and member of the ASE, opened his campaign in South Leeds at Hunslet Mechanics' Institute on the night of 5 July 1895, to the tune of Edward Carpenter's 'England Arise'. From this point on the assumption of the Liberal Party that the working-class interest was identical with its own could no longer be taken for granted. A new definition of political priority was being raised by a section of organized labour. Shaw declared that:

> [He had] formerly belonged to the Liberal Party, and once imagined that it was a great progressive party [Laughter]. But he had found them out and the one thing which enabled him to do so was the experience he had of them during the gas strike in Leeds. When he saw what occurred in connection with that strike he came to the conclusion that if these men were friends of labour it was time the workers reconsidered their position.[38]

Significantly, Irish Catholic political interest was also moving towards the ILP, and the Revd A. H. Kennedy of All Saints Church, York Road, in the centre of the Leeds Irish area, came out in support of Shaw.

The signs that were evident at parliamentary level in 1895 were apparent even earlier in municipal elections. From November 1888 working-class Liberal wards, such as New Wortley, Bramley, Holbeck and Armley and Wortley began to go Conservative; at the same time, South and Headingley wards, from being predominantly Liberal in allegiance, turned predominantly Conservative. In 1894 the Liberal Party recovered in the working-class wards, but in 1895 the Conservatives again captured Liberal strongholds south of the river, and for the first time in 60 years took control of the municipal council.

The wave of new unionist strikes in Leeds from 1889 to 1891, and particularly the strike of employees at the municipal gasworks in the winter of 1889 and the summer of 1890, under socialist leadership, introduced new issues into local politics. Unable to cope with changing aspirations amongst the working-class electorate and the expansion of new unionism, the Liberal Party in Leeds was in trouble by 1895. Roberts has explained the decline as follows:

> The Liberal Party was ill-equipped to deal with the restless and often incoherent aspirations of the working classes. Its response was at best half-hearted, at worst negative. Furthermore, whenever the party made halting overtures to the working classes it only succeeded in alienating some of its middle class supporters.[39]

In the event, the Liberal Party in Leeds did attempt to respond to the symptoms of decline – the electoral setbacks, particularly at municipal level – and to repair its relationship with the labour leaders of the town, particularly after the appearance of an ILP candidate (William Cockayne of the Gasworkers' and General Labourers' Union) in the municipal election in East Hunslet in November 1891. Both ILP and Lib–Lab groups supported Cockayne, Judge and the Lib–Labs on the LTC, acting in an attempt to force the Liberal Party to run candidates who were sympathetic to the labour movement in working-class wards.

The Liberal Party, under the direction of J. S. Mathers as an election organizer, did strive to gain for itself a more progressive image in its dealings with labour. In November 1892 Mathers met the leaders of the LTC to assure them that the party had plans for labour representation. He wished to bring about a more formal federation between local labour and the Liberals 'and to stop before it took any definite form the Labour Party from going off'.[40] William Marston, president of the LTC for much of the 1880s, became a Justice of the Peace, and municipal seats were found in the following years for the strongest Liberals on the LTC. Marston served as a Lib–Lab councillor in the West ward from 1897 to 1912; James Tetley, active in and president of the LICS, as well as an LTC and ASE member, represented East Hunslet from 1897 until 1909; and Owen Connellan, secretary of the LTC and member of the Typographical Association, was a Lib–Lab councillor for East Ward from 1895 until 1904. Thus, the initiatives made by Mathers in 1891–2 took between five and eight years to materialize in the form of real places for representatives of labour within the Liberal Party.

Liberal radicals of the 1850s, 1860s and 1870s, with a Chartist or co-operative background, had recognized that there was a real division of interest between labour and capital and that there was a consequent and recurrent tendency towards social and industrial conflict. They had concentrated their political energies on developing policies for unity in the economic structure of society, which might preserve the harmony between liberalism and labour in the sphere of politics. This political emphasis amounted to a coherent ideology, which the Leeds Liberals lost in the 1880s. Local Liberal politicians did not grasp that new bases for political loyalty and understanding had to be developed in order to meet the expanding and increasingly well-defined demands of labour. The result was that the Liberals turned merely to tactical questions – how to capture the Labour Party, as Mathers put it. Those labour leaders in Leeds who remained sympathetic to the Liberal Party were left with neither a rationale nor a programme for attaching the rest of the growing labour movement to the party in the changed political conditions of the 1890s.

It is clear that the quality of radical liberal ideas changed after the death of the MP R. M. Carter. Following financial difficulties, Carter resigned his seat in Parliament in 1876, effectively dropped out of political life and died six years later in 1882. The man who replaced him, John Barran, did not have the close association with the working-class community enjoyed by Carter, and did not place his emphasis on labour politics. Following the departure of Carter, the *Leeds Express* continued to advocate working-class causes, but the innovative radical approach characteristic of the paper in the period when Lloyd Jones and Carter were involved, was diluted. Yet, paradoxically, J. S. Mathers, who kept Herbert Gladstone informed about the temper of Leeds, and particularly of West Leeds, himself recognized that labour, industrial, and social questions would be the most important ones for the Liberal Party locally to face. Even the Irish question, which dominated Liberal politics between 1886 and 1895, had a labour dimension. In June 1881 Mathers wrote to Gladstone to say that there was a feeling of indifference on Irish questions amongst the rank and file: 'amounting almost to an anti-Irish feeling ... for it is a common saying among working men that if it is to be "Ireland for the Irishmen" then it must be England for Englishmen, whose labour is reduced in value on account of so many Irishmen coming over here'.[41]

The Irish problem was a priority in English politics partly because Gladstone was interested in it and partly, for working-class liberals, because a more settled Ireland might reduce the number of Irish immigrants to towns like Leeds. Mathers saw problems looming for the Liberal Party not so much on big issues such as Ireland as on trends emerging locally. He was deeply disturbed by the series of reverses in the local elections which had culminated in November in 1895 in the Tory capture of the Leeds Council:

> Our organisations, which many seek to lay the blame on, have faults, but there is a deeper current of Toryism here than I have ever known ... so far as I am able to read the signs we shall be found, in a not very distant future, under the flag of a democratic Toryism, or a thoughtful Christian socialism ... The interests of many thousands of employers of labour are now being touched by the labour questions and like all other classes whose interests have been meddled with they are resenting it, most of them talking diluted Toryism and many going right over.[42]

Partly, it was a question of entrenched Liberal interests in the local associations being unwilling to allow labour a direct representation in their wards. After the gas strike there was a series of attempts by labour leaders to get themselves elected as Lib–Labs, and it took a number of years before even a small degree of success was attained. Henry Maundrill, of the Yorkshire Miners' Association and the LTC stood for Holbeck in 1891 and for West Hunslet in 1892, but on both occasions – as a

Lib–Lab challenging the official Liberal – he failed to gain selection by the ward association. Each time he came a very poor third. Similarly John Childerson of the ASE fought West Hunslet in 1891 as a Lib–Lab candidate and was defeated by the official Liberal; when he contested Holbeck in 1893, a safe Liberal ward, he found himself opposed by an ILP candidate – the Conservatives won the seat.

When the first crop of ILP candidates came out in the years following the 1890 gas strike in Leeds, the reaction of the Liberals was, from the beginning, hostile. Mathers attributed the narrow majority of 184 votes gained over the Tory in the Hunslet election of 1891 to the fact that the Liberals had concentrated all their energy against the ILP candidate. Joseph Henry, the radical Liberal in West Leeds, thought that the ILP could only be dealt with belligerently: '... the ILP are shaking and the policy of fighting them is the right one, they will never work with the Liberals and therefore we ought always to treat them as enemies'.[43]

But even Mathers does not appear to have taken his own forebodings too seriously. He did not regard the strengthening current of Toryism, which he recognized in Leeds from the early 1890s, as the result of a wholesale transfer of the working-class vote to Toryism; on the whole, he thought that the vote of the organized and respectable labour move-ment was staying with the Liberal Party. Thus, in the municipal election a year after the gas strike, the gas workers who lived in New Wortley, voted, according to Mather's impression, for the successful Liberal candidate, Thomas Leuty.[44]

In the general election of 1892 Herbert Gladstone's majority was drastically reduced by his Tory opponent, Arthur Greenwood, whose engineering works were, like those of the Liberal James Kitson, also in the West Leeds constituency. Mathers explained the reduced Liberal majority not by the desertion of the respectable organized labour vote, but by the Tory adoption of the method of bribery of the less respectable working class:

> The chief Tory support came from a class of voters inert since 1874. This class is under the influence of the public house and the class of labour or no labour which it pursues, which cares little for wife, child, or home. We must adapt some means to reach this public house class. It is not reached directly by any moral or religious agency. Some mission mixed with politics will have to be set on foot.[45]

In general, the local Liberal Party managers thought that W. E. Gladstone was as right about labour matters as he was about most other questions. Thus, Mathers wrote to Herbert Gladstone fully approving a speech made by his father at West Calder on 23 October 1890. Although

Gladstone stressed that Ireland was 'the greatest by far of all questions', he thought the labour question important enough to devote most of his speech to it. Besides emphasizing the progress made by the working classes under free trade, in political, educational, and trade-union rights, Gladstone pointed to the power of organized labour:

> You will have temptation, gentlemen, you, the labouring people of this country, when you become supreme to such a degree that there is no other power to balance and counteract the power which you possess. You have approaching you, together with great physical, social and political advantages – you have approaching you a deep and searching moral trial ... and when you have become stronger than the capitalist, stronger than the peerage, stronger than the landed gentry, than the great mercantile classes – when you have become in one sense their political master, you have still before you one achievement to fulfil, one glory to attain, and appropriate to yourselves – continue to be just. [Loud cheers].

To be just in Gladstone's terms meant not to act according to class interest, but in the interests of the nation as a whole. He particularly warned against the use of state or parliamentary power in the interests of class: '... one of the most useful and valuable means of strengthening the position of the labouring class without doing harm to any man is what is called the method of co-operation', which tended to promote the principles of independence and self-government. Acts of Parliament could also be used to promote the interests of the labouring class, but he warned:

> ... be slow to interfere with methods which promote liberty [Hear, hear]. An Act of Parliament comes chiefly into competition with the method of combination. While control by Act of Parliament is not necessarily to be dismissed, the achievement of labour interests is far better attained by the act of voluntary combination, which is a greater guarantee of freedom.[46]

To the Liberals in Leeds, this was 'a glorious speech, the right thing to say on labour matters at the right time'.[47] Herbert Gladstone was, in later years, to be responsible for engineering the terms of a national electoral accommodation with a rising Labour Party. That this was done without attempting to analyse the philosophical and political grounds on which the labour movement might associate with the Liberal Party was a major factor in the slow decay of the Liberal Party, both in Leeds and nationally.

Notes

1. Viscount Gladstone Papers 46039, 9 November 1895.
2. A. Roberts, *The Liberal Party in West Yorkshire 1885–1895*, Ph.D. thesis (University of Leeds, 1979), p. 48.
3. H. J. Hanham, *Elections and Party Management* (London, 1959), p. 327.
4. K. Laybourn and J. Reynolds, *Liberalism and the Rise of Labour 1890–1918*, (London, 1987), pp. 44–5.
5. *Leeds Trades Council Minutes, (LTC Mins.)* 5 July 1882.
6. *LTC Mins.*, 4 April 1883.
7. *LTC Mins.*, 12 December 1888 and 28 February 1890.
8. T. Mann, 'What a Compulsory Eight Hour Working Day Means to the Workers', (1886), *Reprints in Labour History* 2 (London, 1972), introduction by R. Hyman.
9. *LTC Mins.*, 7 December 1887.
10. *LTC Mins.*, 7 February and 5 November 1883.
11. *LTC Mins.*, 4 April 1883.
12. Hanham, *Elections and Party Management*, ch. 15.
13. *LTC Mins*, 4 March 1885.
14. *LTC Mins.*, 14 November 1890. Gladstone to Trades Council.
15. For an account of the career of Dilke, see G. M. Tuckwell, *A Short Life of Sir Charles W. Dilke* (London, 1925).
16. *Industrial Remuneration Conference Report* (London, 1885), p. 4.
17. L. T. Hobhouse, *The Labour Movement* (1893), p. 41.
18. M. Freeden, *The New Liberalism: An Ideology of Social Reform* (Oxford, 1978).
19. *IRC Report*, pp. 435–7.
20. *Ibid.*, p. 502.
21. The Labour Co-Partnership Movement aimed 'to bring about an organisation of industry based on Labour Co-Partnership, that is to say, a system in which all those engaged shall share in the profit, capital, control and responsibility', and worked to extend the organization of all forms of production under the co-operative system. The movement originated with the Labour Association for the Promotion of Co-operative Production, formed at the Derby Co-operative Congress in 1884. The name of the organization was subsequently shortened to the Labour Co-Partnership Association, which produced the monthly journal *Co-Partnership*. See H. Vivian, 'Co-Partnership in Practice', Labour Co-Partnership Association (May, 1914).
22. B. Potter, *The Co-Operative Movement in Great Britain* (London, 1904).
23. Numbers employed by the Co-operative Wholesale Society in manufacturing occupations in Leeds (1897) were as follows (total 541):

	Profit (£)	Wages (£)	Nos. employed	Date commenced
Corn mill	7,300	2,700	33	1847
Bakery	790	1,207	18	1879

Bespoke clothing	1,100	3,100	51	?
Boot and shoe	2,400	7,600	168	1873
Brush factory	214	710	10	1888
Cabinet-making	1	405	34	1895
Millinery	1,100	264	10	1881
Dressmaking	94	366	24	1895
Building	?	12,000	193	1875

Source: G. J. Holyoake, *Jubilee History of the Leeds Industrial Co-operative Society* (Manchester, 1897), p. 257.

24. *Royal Commission on Labour (RCL)*, 1893–4, PP, XXXIX, Pt. 1, Q. 56–61, pp. 13–14.

25. *RCL*, Q. 213, p. 22, and Q. 222, p. 22. For more evidence on this see B. Jones, *Co-Operative Production* I and II (Oxford, 1894). Mitchell also had doubts about the use of trade-union funds to finance co-operative enterprise; see *RCL*, Q. 182. p. 20.

26. See *Leeds Co-operative Record*, November 1899.

27. See the biographies of, for example, Fawcett, Gaunt, Bell, Tetley, Thornton, Leach, Dockeray, Earnshaw and Wilberforce in Holyoake, *Jubilee History*, pp. 219–30.

28. *Ibid.*, p. 223.

29. *Leeds Mercury*, 25 November 1885.

30. James Kitson to Herbert Gladstone, 4 April 1885, Viscount Gladstone Papers (VGP), British Museum Add. MS. 46027.

31. *Leeds Mercury*, 25 November 1885.

32. *Yorkshire Post*, 24 November 1910.

33. *Leeds Mercury*, 18 November 1885.

34. Leuty has been described by Roberts as 'a highly promising politician with a keen social conscience'. A woollen manufacturer, a congregationalist, and Lord Mayor in 1894, he firmly expressed support for working-class aspirations. Roberts, *The Liberal Party*, p. 198; and *Yorkshire Post*, 4 April 1895.

35. *Yorkshire Post*, 22 April 1895.

36. *Ibid.*, 26 April 1895.

37. *Ibid.*, 29 April and 1 May 1895.

38. *Ibid.*, 6 July 1895.

39. Roberts, *The Liberal Party*, p. 175.

40. Mathers to Gladstone, 20 November 1892, VGP, 46039.

41. *Ibid.*, 10 June 1881.

42. *Ibid.*, 19 November 1895.

43. Joseph Henry to Gladstone, 14 March 1897, VGP, 46036.

44. Mathers to Gladstone, 25 November 1891, VGP, 46039.

45. *Ibid.*, 21 July 1892.

46. *The Times*, 24 October 1890.

47. Mathers to Gladstone, 25 October 1890, VGP, 46039. For further discussion on W. E. Gladstone's attitude to social legislation, see M. Barker, *Gladstone and Radicalism* (Hassocks/Sussex, 1975), p. 195 *passim*.

Chapter 3

Socialists: Organizations and Ideas, 1884–1890 [1]

A definite step is now being taken towards the formation of a socialist Labour Party in Leeds. In all our large towns and in all civilised countries a similar movement is gathering force and whenever there is enlightenment among working men, there is also socialism. The objects of socialism are, briefly, to make life easy for all who are willing to do their fair share of work, to put a stop to the mad competition for existence which is the cause of poverty on all hands, and to establish a co-operative commonwealth by restoring the means of production to their proper owners – the people …

Tom Maguire, Handbill of the Leeds Socialist League, 1887. [1]

The revival of socialism

In the mid-1880s socialist activity in Leeds was limited to the pioneering activities of a small group of street propagandists, numbering fewer than ten. By 1909 forty-seven different trade unions and a total of sixteen political associations (including ward Labour representation committees, ILP and socialist clubs, and Women's Labour League branches), representing a total membership of 11,232, were affiliated to the Leeds Labour Representation Committee (LLRC). In this growth of independent labour and socialist politics the political culture of Leeds was transformed. While the Liberal Party looked secure in its domination of the parliamentary constituencies, the basis of that strength was being eroded in the local wards; by 1913 the Labour Party had more elected councillors than the Liberal Party in the city. The following chapters trace how the transformation occurred.

A serious defect of the Liberal Party in Leeds was its failure take on board philosophically, or to apply in practice, the progressive views developed either by their MP, R. M. Carter (the ideas of co-operative communalism) or by those Liberals who advocated a local and national

46

welfare state. Into the void stepped a new generation of socialist pioneers. In Leeds (and most industrial centres had their equivalents) two men were important in the revival of socialist thinking: Tom Maguire (1864–95) and John Lincoln Mahon (1865–1933).[2] Maguire was a photographer's assistant, Mahon was a skilled engineer, and both were at the forefront of political activity in Leeds at a crucial transitional point.

Maguire was born on 28 December 1864, the son of Frances and John Maguire, at 3 Saint Street, Leeds. Little is known about his early years, except that his father, who was a journeyman marble polisher, died during Maguire's boyhood. His parents were Irish Catholic immigrants and he was actively brought up in the Catholic faith, singing in the Cathedral choir, as Edward Carpenter writing in *Justice*, the paper of the Socialist Democratic Federation (SDF), later recalled.[3] He read widely in theology, but then began to be influenced by freethinking and secularist ideas. His first contact with socialism occurred when he came across a copy of the *Christian Socialist* newspaper at the Secular Hall bookstall. *Justice* was available in Leeds probably from February 1884.

During the 1880s, as the country struggled to come to terms with the depression which had set in in the late 1870s, a great deal of attention was being devoted to the discovery of poverty in the centres of the large industrial cities. The speeches and writings of Henry George (the American classical political economist) did much to raise a national debate about the causes of poverty in which the ideas of socialism became more clearly defined.[4] The revival of interest in socialist ideas in Leeds was strongly influenced by events in London, and does not appear to be the result of a resurgence of a latent local socialism. Leeds Chartism had followed a moderate path and had developed to form a radical strand within the Liberal Party. Socialism, when it re-emerged after the radical activities of the 1830s and 1840s, was taken up by a small group of individuals predominantly from the Leeds Irish community, amongst whom Maguire was the most talented and influential.

By late 1883, at the age of nineteen, Maguire was speaking at Vicar's Croft in Leeds, arguing from the text 'Socialism Made Plain' issued by the SDF in June 1883. However, it was to be another year before a Leeds branch of the SDF was fully constituted. Regular outdoor meetings and speeches throughout the summer of 1884 built up an interested audience, and by September 1884 Maguire could gather an assembly of 300 people to hear a lecture on 'The Aims of Socialism' which asserted the social class unity of working people. At the same time, John Mahon made his first appearance in Leeds and, at 16 Henbury Street, he and Maguire together founded a Leeds branch of the SDF, with Maguire as its secretary. By October, the branch numbered 25 members and the following two months were spent in a series of propaganda meetings, held in the hope of encouraging the transition of working-class radicals from the Liberal Party to the SDF.[5] To a point, this was successful, but the major influence on the membership of the SDF locally was the personal following of Maguire. As one pioneer member later recalled:

> I was a frequenter to Vicar's Croft [Leeds] in the years 1883–1884. At that time I was a follower of Charles Bradlaugh and the Radical school ... There was a branch of the SDF in Leeds. I remember Tom Maguire and a few friends and I believe they came mainly from St Ann's Roman Catholic Church.[6]

During the three and a half months of its existence, the Leeds SDF remained small. Beyond the half dozen or so friends of Maguire, the active membership had expanded by early January 1885 to include two or three engineers, one of whom was Alfred Mattison who spent much of his time recording the development of the movement between 1885 and his death in 1944. Also included in their number was Matt Sollitt who promoted anarchist ideas and parted company when the socialists moved towards electoral politics; as an advocate of the revolutionary general strike, he declared that 'every time a man votes at election times he is admitting his incapacity to govern himself'.[7]

In Leeds the SDF barely had time to digest and develop, let alone propagate basic socialist ideas, before its national leadership in London split. By 1883–4 the leaders of the socialist movement had broadly agreed on what constituted a theory of socialism,[8] but there was confusion on the question of how best to achieve their goals in a mass working-class movement. Discontent with the leadership of H. M. Hyndman, in particular, had built up so much that, by the middle of December, a challenge had been initiated. Mahon, who had helped Maguire to set up the Leeds SDF only two and a half months previously, was involved in the cabal, which also included William Morris, Eleanor Marx, Edward Aveling and E. B. Bax. The clash was partly one of personalities, centring on Hyndman's alleged self-promoting manner, and in part the outcome of a strategic disagreement about the role of parliamentary reforms or 'stepping stones' on the road to socialism. William Morris provided the leadership for another perspective – which would lead to the Utopia described in his *News from Nowhere* (1890) – seeking a pure revolution without getting involved in electoral politics. The Leeds branch followed Morris, less because of the strategic debate and more because of the personal friendship which was growing up between Mahon and Maguire. The challenge to Hyndman's leadership led not to his ousting, but to the departure of the dissidents and the formation of a new organization, the Socialist League – on 30 December 1884. The beliefs of the new group were set out in the Manifesto of the Socialist League.[9]

The news of the split in the SDF leadership reached Leeds sometime in late December 1884, in a letter to Tom Maguire from John Mahon. Maguire made clear his apprehension about the consequences of the secession. He was worried about the account presented to him of the dispute. Why did well-known leaders, such as J. L. Joynes, John Burns, H. H. Champion and Harry Quelch, not side with the seceders? Since they did not desert the SDF:

> ... the Socialist League will then have to fight against something like an equality of intellect and influence and the result will be that some branches will declare for you, some for the 'Fed.' and that the people will be more or less divided by the very science whose backbone is unity.[10]

By late January 1885 the Leeds SDF branch was still requesting information and had not made up its mind which way it would move. The result was crippling uncertainty in Leeds and a marked fall-off in confidence, enthusiasm and membership. Early in February 1885 Maguire wrote accusingly to Mahon that his branch was left with only twelve members. At this point Mahon acted and dispatched himself, as secretary of the Socialist League, to address the Leeds SDF on the causes of the split. This meeting took place on the evening of Sunday 8 February in the Royal Sovereign Inn on Vicar Lane, when Mahon justified the position of the Socialist League to the eighteen members present:

> In conclusion I stated that if the branch resolved to dissolve itself and the meeting then became a branch of the Socialist League they must clearly understand that such a resolution involved the renunciation of the political opportunism and State Socialism of the SDF and a full endorsement of the purely revolutionary propaganda to which the Socialist League was pledged ... This position they accepted at once and seemed to be fully aware of the difference of principle.[11]

Consequently, it was resolved 'that this branch of the SDF be declared dissolved and that henceforward this body be described as the Leeds branch of the Socialist League'.[12] Six people were elected to form a committee (Reilly, Finn, Woolley, Malone, Connell and McHale) in addition to Maguire and Corkwell (secretaries) and Kelly (treasurer). The group was made up of a small band of enthusiasts, with Maguire, Kelly and Sollitt doing most of the speaking, and a total of twelve constituting the active membership of the branch, which Mahon considered to be very inexperienced in the methods of political propaganda and organization.

The Socialist League

In his earliest political statements Maguire had advocated practical socialism, stressing the need for immediate reforms – for example, a legislated eight-hour day. From March 1885, however, this approach was abandoned in favour of the revolutionary politics advocated by William Morris and the Socialist League in the pages of the League's newspaper, *Commonweal*. The objective was the complete conversion, through persistent propaganda and education, to 'the cause'. The task was to make socialists. Street propaganda was seen as the main method of spreading the cause, and strikes and industrial disputes were opportunities to develop revolutionary class-consciousness. The spring and summer of 1885 found the new Socialist League enthusiastically preaching to the miners locked out in the collieries around Leeds: 'it was thought that if, by an effort, we could shed a little light on their darkness "the cause" in general would be the better for it. Colliers, like most men, no doubt realise socialism better on empty stomachs than on full ones ...' Evidently, the colliers did not agree: '... our collier agitation scheme did not strike fire and as they did not seem the sort of men for such an understanding we did not press the matter.'[13]

On 1 July 1885 six women were killed in Leeds when part of a nail factory collapsed. Maguire used the event to attack the ameliorative approach to such problems, on the grounds that the Employers' Liability Acts and other similar measures dealt with effects, not with causes. Members of the Socialist League continued to insist on the need to convert people to socialism rather than to extend trade-unionism. A strong belief in the imminence of socialism and the realization of 'the cause' seems to have sustained the activists in their public commitment. Privately, however, Maguire expressed frustration at the small impact and slow growth of the Socialist League. The normal round of municipal electioneering was, it seems, capable of stirring more passions amongst working people than socialist speechmongering. Late in 1885 and early in 1886, Maguire began to notice a growing interest in political questions (i.e. an interest in representation in the formal civic and national institutions) within the organized labour movement. A Labour Electoral Committee had been set up in 1886, following the 1885 TUC conference, and this had developed by 1887 into the Labour Electoral Association, influenced by H. H. Champion.[14] Initially, the Socialist League in Leeds viewed such developments negatively. It could not, however, ignore the existence of an interest in reform through the political system. Maguire expressed his view in a letter to Mahon:

> ... political reform with the intelligent worker of my acquaintance seems to be the great end of all organisation. Experience leads me to believe that such is the prevailing idea with the generality of men. Working men's and parliamentary representation societies are being formed all over Yorkshire and with much enthusiasm too. In Leeds, Bradford ... and elsewhere trade unions are taking the matter up and everywhere there seems to be a predisposition in favour of

bettering the world and its inhabitants by Act of Parliament. These
societies will keep many a good fellow out of our ranks this coming
summer ...[15]

In September 1886 the Fabian Society declared itself in favour of parliamentary action and organized a three-day conference to debate the
merits of parliamentary and revolutionary action. Morris, the main
influence on the Socialist League, cautioned strongly against developing
a parliamentary Labour Party on the lines, for example, of the Irish
Nationalist Party.[16] Leeds clearly followed William Morris:

> We are convinced that any alliance of radicals or social reformers as
> such, and Socialists, in order to work from a common basis would be
> detrimental to the weaker and more advanced section and we cannot
> understand how a socialist body can enter into such a compact with-
> out compromise of principle.[17]

However, a second fruitless winter followed for the members of the
Leeds Socialist League, and by March 1887 a marked political change
had occurred, indicated by their reaction to a strike of engineers at
Fowler's Engineering Company. Significantly, the League supported
the case of the men against piece-work, whereas six months previously
they would have criticized the relevance of trade-union issues and
appealed for conversion to an ill-defined socialism. At the annual conference of the Socialist League, held in May 1887, the Leeds branch
voted with the minority parliamentary group, and by the autumn of
the same year Maguire was speaking on the need to develop a Labour
Party.[18] In 1918, looking back on the history of the local Labour Party,
the *Leeds Weekly Citizen* recognized the germ of the party in the handbill
issued in 1887 by the Socialist League, and written by Maguire, which
heralded the intention of the socialists to move more closely to the
immediate concerns of independent labour politics and trade-union
struggles. There had clearly occurred a change of approach from the
politics of conversion to the politics of intervention.

The change in emphasis undoubtedly brought fresh confidence and
new support to the Socialist League, which had reported in July 1887
that 'a growing sympathy with socialism is perceptible in this town';[19]
there was an increase in membership from among the Jewish tailors
following the 1888 strike; and the branch was commenting on well-
attended meetings at Vicar's Croft. By September 1887 the Leeds branch
had decided on a course of development separate from London and the
Commonweal:

> At our last weekly branch meeting it was decided to stop taking the
> *Commonweal*. We owe a good sum and until we pay it we are simply

tying a millstone around our necks. The *Commonweal* is a dead failure around here and excepting the few we purchase at the branch, never circulates.[20]

By the summer of 1889 the branch was active and buoyant. Large crowds attended its outdoor meetings, and it was, consequently, well placed to take advantage of the wave of strikes that began in the autumn of 1889 amongst the unskilled and semi-skilled workers and which led to the period of new unionism.[21] By mid-1889 the Socialist League was breaking up; the branches at Glasgow, Leicester, Norwich, and Yarmouth were coming under anarchist influence, while those at Leeds, Bradford, Manchester and Aberdeen were all moving towards parliamentary action and were increasingly acting independently of the national organization. The Leeds branch began to turn for influence and information to Champion's *Labour Elector*, and to the newly published (1889) *Yorkshire Factory Times*. By March 1890, shortly after William Morris had lectured in Leeds on 'The Class Struggle', the branch fell apart after a fundamental disagreement about the political significance of the new union strikes between the anarchist and 'parliamentary' groups within the organization. Two members of the anarchist group were active in Leeds between 1890 and 1892. George Cores had organized a large meeting in Leeds to commemorate the Chicago anarchists, and spoke about the relationship between communist anarchism and revolutionary violence. At the same time *Commonweal* had come under the control of the revolutionary anarchists. The editorial of 1 November 1890, entitled 'Revolutionary Warfare', had argued that 'every act of lawlessness is the preliminary to the social revolution' and that 'Whatever weapons the workers find at hand it is their duty to use'.[22] There was little support in Leeds for such views. The manner in which the labour movement and socialist politics were to develop in the city over the period 1888–95 is best illustrated through a further consideration of the political interests and ideas of Maguire, and particularly of Mahon.

John Lincoln Mahon and Leeds socialism

In his biography of William Morris E. P. Thompson has described the entry of Mahon into socialist politics and his emergence as one of the best socialist theoreticians of the labour movement, particularly in his writings about the relationship between socialism and the labour movement as a whole.[23] In Thompson's account Mahon came to have less influence than people like Tom Mann, but in Leeds his influence was crucial. John Lincoln Mahon was born in Edinburgh in 1865. His father, who was Irish, was a skilled engine fitter and Mahon learnt the trade of marine engineering in his father's workshop. Little is known about the influences that awakened his interest in socialist ideas, but his earliest correspondence indicates that, like Maguire, he was affected by the debate between Hyndman and Bradlaugh on the relationship between land reform and socialism. As early as March 1884 Mahon, then only in his nineteenth year, had corresponded with Morris in order to arrange lectures by him in Edinburgh and to get advice on forming a socialist organization there. In May 1884 he decided that the best course of action would be to form an organization which would incorporate labour and land questions, a project which Morris knew held dangers, particularly the fear that interest in land reform would make a side issue of what both regarded as the fundamental question – that of socialism and its critique of industrial capitalism. However, Morris felt that as long as the new organization, the Scottish Land and Labour League, was in the hands of both Mahon and Andreas Scheu, who had arrived in Edinburgh to help Mahon, it would be the best way of promoting socialist ideas in the Scottish context.

Mahon, however, in making this move had unwittingly taken a step that, within six months, was to bring him into greater prominence as a figure within the developing socialist movement nationally. Hyndman, the founder of the SDF was against the Scottish Land and Labour League idea from the start and this, along with his personal attacks on its co-promoters, Mahon and Scheu, was to precipitate the split in the SDF in December 1884. In the meantime Mahon set up a bookshop in Edinburgh, which failed after a few months, and he then travelled in search of alternative work, arriving in Leeds in the summer of 1884, and remaining there probably until late November 1884, while Andreas Scheu carried on the Land and Labour League agitation in Scotland. While in Leeds, Mahon made contact with Maguire, and it was after a series of talks by them that the Leeds branch of the SDF was founded. By the autumn of 1884 Mahon had also started a correspondence with Engels, an association which was to be deeply influential in the formation and maturation of Mahon's political ideas.

On 27 December 1884 Mahon attended the council meeting of the SDF and voted with the majority of ten who then seceded to form the Socialist League. At the age of twenty, Mahon became the national secretary of the provisional council of the new Socialist League, whose constitution expressed the following four objectives:

(1)   Forming and helping other socialist bodies to form a National and International Socialist Labour Party.
(2)   Striving to conquer political power by promoting the election of socialists to local governments, Schools Boards, and other administrative bodies.
(3)   Helping Trade Unionism, Co-operation, and every genuine movement for the good of the workers.

(4) Promoting a scheme for the National and International Federation of Labour.[24]

This constitution was dropped at the first annual conference of the
League in favour of the anti-parliamentary position of Morris, and Mahon set about persuading the Leeds SDF branch to join the League.

Mahon's position as secretary of the Socialist League lasted for only
four months, from January until May 1885. He presented his resignation in a letter of 4 May 1885, with the remark that it was 'quite
evident that we do not get on together as well as a Secretary and Council
should'.[25] In the late autumn of 1885 Mahon moved again to Leeds where
he remained until towards the end of the following year, during which
time both he and the branch stuck faithfully to the revolutionary propaganda of the League. Though he had moved back into the engineering
trade in Leeds, Mahon took no part in ordinary trade-union activity,
except to attack it, nor did he participate directly in the activities of the
Leeds branch, leaving this to Maguire. He used the time to write for
Commonweal and to extend the influence of the Socialist League in
Yorkshire and beyond. His attitude sprang directly from what he took
to be the meaning of the first volume of Marx's *Das Kapital*:

> Now that they [the workers] are feeling the pinch more keenly, they
> would become more intelligent. So long as English capitalists have a
> monopoly of the world's markets the workers might never become
> miserable enough to make revolution a necessity ... but our trade is
> now declining ... capitalists struggle to decrease wages ... and this
> hastens the destruction of the system ...[26]

Mahon's view of trade unions was simply that their actions could either
be revolutionary, or irrelevant and impotent. There was no middle
ground. He made scathing attacks on the deliberations of the Hull
Trades Council and the 1886 TUC conference at Hull for what he
saw as their muddled involvement in Liberal politics. The speech of
F. Maddison, in support of more political representation along Lib–Lab
lines, he characterized as 'remarkably advanced for a trade unionist and
remarkably backward for a socialist'. This purist view of socialist politics
was explained to the Leeds branch by Mahon and loyally followed
by them for the two years 1885–7, and was clearly outlined by Morris
in one of the earliest issues of *Commonweal*:

> I should like our friend to understand whither the whole system of
> palliation tends – namely, to the creation of a new middle class to
> act as a buffer between the proletariat and their direct and obvious
> masters; the only hope of the bourgeois for retarding the advance of
> socialism lies in this device. Shall the ultimate end of civilization be

the perpetual widening of the middle classes? I think if our friend knew as well as I do the terrible mental degradation of our middle classes, their hypocrisy, their joylessness, it would scare him from attempting to use their beloved instrument of amelioration – Parliament ...

If by chance any good is to be got out of the legislation of the ruling classes, the necessary concessions are much more likely to be wrung out of them by fear ... than they are to be wheedled and coaxed out of them by the continued life of compromise which 'parliamentary socialists' would be compelled to live, and which is deadly to that feeling of exalted hope and brotherhood that alone can hold a revolutionary party together.[27]

In March 1887 Mahon went to Northumberland to campaign amongst the locked-out miners. His experiences there began a series of adjustments of his political views. During the campaign, Mahon fashioned three new ideas which he was to apply over the following seven years. Firstly, he saw the necessity for a united socialist Labour Party, which he anticipated would emerge as a result of pressure from the North and Scotland. Secondly, he changed course, in the sense that he no longer expected trade-unionists and others active in the labour movement to hand in their cards and transfer to a revolutionary socialist party; rather, he advocated that socialists should enter labour organizations and gain positions of leadership in them. Thirdly, he began to suggest that just as there was a midway position between the standoffish purism of the Socialist League and the Lib–Labism of trade union leaders, there could be a similar midway position in political activity, where political organizations might be used to display socialist ideas and force a socialist transition.

Mahon switched sides at the May 1887 annual meeting of the Socialist League, when a provision for activity in parliamentary politics was formulated as the main opposition resolution. In the event, the resolution was lost and for the second time in his young career Mahon was at the centre of a split within a socialist organization – it was from this point that the Socialist League did indeed begin to break up, as Morris had warned Mahon it would. Morris had also warned Mahon that his new ideas about organization and programme were rather vague, as indeed they were in the spring of 1887. Mahon spent the summer and autumn of 1887, after the defeat of the Northumberland miners, in an attempt to clarify his ideas on the relationship between socialism and the labour movement. He began this investigation in a series of articles in *Commonweal*, in which he attempted more fully to establish what the role of labour politics and trade-union action in socialist politics should be:

Socialism is simply the most advanced stage of the labour movement. It aims at changing the present system of society. The Socialist Party has no interests in antagonism to other labour organisations ... they fight for the interest of a part of the people, while socialism aims at the good of all ... trades unionism means securing to the workers a larger share of the fruits of their labour; socialism means securing to the workers the full fruits of their labour ... the very gist of the socialist policy is to combine all sectional labour movements into one solid array with a clearly defined aim ... In thus trying to conciliate other working class organizations, let it be understood that I am not in the least wishful to compromise the socialist aim. I don't wish socialists to turn mere reformers, but to make reformers socialists.[28]

Mahon outlined a policy which was to be dominant amongst Leeds socialists from 1888:

They should struggle to get socialists elected to various Trades Councils, they should send more socialists to the Trades Congress, they should organize a distinct section there and make war upon the Burt and Broadhurst gang who now use trade unionism as a tool for the Liberal Party.[29]

Never a man to mince his words, Mahon was fully prepared to 'raise the devil' in the heart of the organized labour movement, a policy which the LTC was to taste in future years. He wrote to Engels on 14 January 1888, informing him that he had returned from Scotland to the North of England, where his main preoccupation was again the creation of a united Socialist Party. Now, however, he saw parliamentary action as being central to the scheme of socialist unity:

I am quite certain that there are at least four constituencies where socialist candidates could fight with every chance of success. If we could only manage to get three or four socialist MP's who were good sound fellows we could put socialism in this country on a different footing. Their influence as propagandists would not only spread the principles but enable them to weld the party together.[30]

By 1888 Mahon had left the Socialist League and had helped Keir Hardie to fight the Mid Lanark by-election in March 1888 and to form the Scottish Labour Party. Returning to London, where he stayed in 1889 and 1890, he launched a further organization, the Labour Union, which was an attempt to give expression to the ideas he had formulated in 1888 in his important publication, *A Labour Programme*.[31]

Significantly, Leeds had followed Mahon in his policies. By 1889 they too had effectively broken with the Socialist League. Maguire was one of the signatories to the platform of the Labour Union (1889) and it was these two still young men who were to guide the movement in Leeds through the 'new unionist strikes' of 1889–92 to the formation of the ILP in 1893. Much of the rationale for their actions is provided in Mahon's *A Labour Programme*. For this reason it is necessary to consider its ideas in some detail, because it is not possible to understand the Leeds ILP in its formative years without so doing.

In his introduction to *A Labour Programme* Mahon hinted that his concern had shifted to incorporate the organized labour movement – even the labour aristocracy – which, he argued, was subject to increasing insecurity because of the spread of mechanization. Mahon's programme was an attempt to synthesize the ideas of Morris's League with the aspirations of labour organizations in a way that would lead to a fundamental transformation of economic, social and political relationships. The Marxist concepts of class struggle, of 'wage slavery' and the labour theory of value, run through the analysis presented. British capitalism was threatened by foreign competition and by its own internal contradictions; competition led to a drive for greater productivity which was achieved through mechanization, and this, in turn, displaced labour and led to overproduction and slump: 'Long periods of depression are only varied by periods of unhealthy speculative excitement ... One of these oscillations, perhaps even the present one, will be violent enough to shatter the whole system.'[32]

However, the main interest of the programme lies not in its economic analysis, but in the political strategy which it advanced and the role within this strategy which it provided for labour organization. The goal proposed for socialism was 'simply a scheme of cooperation based upon state-ownership and control of the means of production',[33] in a way which was seen to be revolutionary but was not to be achieved in the total and sudden sense envisaged in the early years in the Socialist League. He cleared the ground by defining 'true' as opposed to 'false' co-operation, and rejected previous experiments in co-operation as being too limited in scale, 'inclined to isolated branches of industry' and 'dependent on realising a profit by dealing in the open market'. Further, 'some concerns at present are called co-operative productive societies although the actual workers have no share whatever in the profits. This is sham co-operation, in which financial success is gained at the expense of principle.'

The type of socialism outlined by Mahon was a curious blend of Owenite co-operation – with elements of what was later to become known as syndicalism – and parliamentary socialism, the whole project motivated by the attempt to find common ground for the 'political' (parliamentary) and the 'non-political' (revolutionary) socialists. The programme advocated setting up a socialist area of production within the economy which would be 'practically independent of the outside

markets, and unaltered by competition'. Mahon judged that this co-
operative wedge could be introduced into society if it was based on a
pioneering group of 10,000 married workmen and their dependents
engaged in the direct production of all their needs. The agency in the
formation of this socialist enclave would be the state, which would
provide the finance and set up the project through a Board of Commissioners, and this would then be replaced by managers elected by the
workers in the co-operative. The scheme was to be a voluntary one: 'It
must be understood that this is not a scheme for dealing specially with
the unemployed or the paupers of the present system. It is a means of
bringing about a permanently equitable distribution of labour and wealth.'
The principle of organization and control in these state co-operatives
offered an alternative to the ideas about state socialism which were
being developed, particularly by the Fabians. Mahon's plan conceded
the need for centralized control, to a degree that might have horrified
Morris, but there was an important recognition of the need for direct
democracy in the co-operatives. With his system of state co-operatives
outlined, Mahon believed they would spread by the voluntary transformation of private enterprise into state-sponsored co-operatives, as
the crisis of capitalist industry intensified and employers realized the
impossibility of making private profit.

Mahon also proceeded to castigate the socialist theories which he had
himself advocated and practised in London and Leeds between 1884
and 1886:

> The 'non-political' Socialists are not less hazy in their aim, and much
> more diverting in their arguments. While the other is all practice,
> they are all theory. Their method is, first, to elaborate a theory of the
> present system; next, to elaborate another theory of the system that
> should be. Then they are forced to proceed with the demonstration
> of the utter contradiction between these two systems and the impos-
> sibility of compromise … In despair you ask how on earth the gap is
> to be got over at all. And the theorist calmly explains that the present
> system will get worse and worse until the crisis comes. When the
> crisis comes the world will be suddenly yanked from the hideous
> depths of commercialism to the glorious heights of socialism.[34]

Mahon had thus become converted to the view that campaigns for the
improvement of conditions could be mounted and, to some degree,
achieved. Socialist transformation would not solely be the outcome of
the revolt of the empty stomach, but was more likely to proceed from a
strong working class than from a desperate one. In an interesting passage
anticipating many of the problems he was to have in Leeds, Mahon
singled out the Liberal Party as the specific object of attack: 'An active
Labour Party must in the first place push aside the nominal labour

representatives in the House of Commons. Next it would detach large bodies of workmen from the Liberal Party ...' The work of the Labour Party is thus summarized by Mahon:

(1)   To educate the people in social and economic questions, and to train them in the use of their power through political and trade organisations.

(2)   To obtain the extension of political power.

(3)   To ameliorate the conditions of the wage-system.

(4)   To obtain the gradual nationalisation of monopolies with the consequent abolition of the wage-system.[35]

However, in his advocacy of constitutional politics Mahon did not separate political from industrial action. Union organization had to be extended to the unskilled as a precondition for the advance of the Labour Party: 'The first step to take in this matter is to organize some general workmen's Union, which all workers, men and women, could join without regard to their occupation. The next step would be to get a workable system of Labour Federation established ...'[36] This re-organization and extension of the trade-union role served two purposes. Federated labour organization would enable the more effective co-ordination of strikes in pursuit of improved pay and conditions. It could also provide a means of forcing the question of socialism on employers and on Parliament – a second edge to political organization. *A Labour Programme*, fashioned from experiences in Leeds and the north of England, presented an imaginative vision for labour and socialist politics which contained elements of the ideas of Owenite socialists blended into a programme of electoral and trade-union politics. It was an affirmation of a long tradition of thinking which believed that the liberty tree needed roots in economic as well as political democracy.

Notes

1.   The wording of the Handbill is reproduced in *Leeds Weekly Citizen*, 14 January 1918.

2.   For a good account of the national context see E. P. Thompson, *William Morris: Romantic to Revolutionary* (London, 1977), and M. Crick, *The History of the Social Democratic Federation* (Keele, 1994).

3.   *Tom Maguire, a Remembrance: being selections from the Prose and Verse Writings of a Socialist Pioneer* (Manchester, 1895) (with memoirs by E. Carpenter and A. Mattison), p. ix.

4.   See J. Saville, 'Henry George and The British Labour Movement: A Select Bibliography with Commentary', *Bulletin of The Society For The Study of Labour History* 5 (Autumn 1962), pp. 18–26.

5.   *Justice*, 27 December 1884.

6.	B. Hill, in A. Mattison, *Notebook* 3, 3 February 1918 (unpublished MSS).
7.	*Leeds Weekly Citizen*, 1 August 1913: see also J. Quail, *The Slow Burning Fuse: The Lost History of the British Anarchists* (London, 1978).
8.	The following account of the development of socialist ideas nationally is based on Thompson, *William Morris*, ch. III. These ideas were defined in H. M. Hyndman, *Socialism Made Plain* (London, 1883), and in H. M. Hyndman and W. Morris, *Summary of The Principles of Socialism* (London, 1884).
9.	The manifesto is reprinted in full in Thompson, *William Morris*, pp. 732–40.
10.	Maguire to Mahon, 30 December 1884, Socialist League Correspondence (SLC) 2122/1.
11.	Report of the delegate to the Leeds branch of the SDF, 8 February 1885, by J. L. Mahon, SLC, 598.
12.	*Commonweal*, March 1885.
13.	Maguire to Mahon, 22 May 1885, SLC, 2129/5.
14.	H. Pelling, *Origins of The Labour Party 1880–1900* (London, 1954), pp. 57–65.
15.	Maguire to Mahon, undated letter (probably early 1886), SLC, 2128.
16.	'Report of the Proceedings of The Three Day Conference', June 1886, cited in Pelling, *Origins of the Labour Party*, pp. 50–1.
17.	Leeds Socialist League to London Socialist League (undated), SLC, 2134/7.
18.	*Commonweal*, 15 October 1887.
19.	*Ibid.*, 16 July 1887.
20.	T. Paylor, Leeds branch secretary, to secretary of London Socialist League, 11 September 1888, SLC, 2417/4.
21.	*Commonweal*, 8 June 1889, reported meetings with between 700 and 1,000 in attendance.
22.	*Ibid.*, 1 November 1890; editorial by D. J. Nicoll. For a good account of anarchist history and ideas, see Quail, *The Slow Burning Fuse*.
23.	Thompson, *William Morris* (1955 edn), pp. 572–3.
24.	*Ibid.*, p. 381.
25.	Letter of 4 May 1885, cited in R. Page Arnot, *William Morris* (London, 1946), p. 52.
26.	'Bad Times', *Commonweal*, April 1886.
27.	'Socialism and Politics', *Commonweal*, July supplement 1885, quoted in Thompson, *William Morris*, pp. 381–2.
28.	'A Labour Policy', *Commonweal*, 25 August 1887.
29.	*Commonweal*, 8 October 1887.
30.	Mahon to Engels, 14 January 1888, in Thompson, *William Morris* (1955), pp. 869–70.
31.	J. L. Mahon, *A Labour Programme* (London, 1888), Labour Platform Series, No. 1.
32.	*Ibid.*, pp. 27–8.
33.	All the following quotations are from *A Labour Programme*.
34.	*Ibid.* p. 63.
35.	*Ibid.*, pp. 74–6.
36.	*Ibid.*, pp 79–80.

Chapter 4

The Formation of the Independent Labour Party

Now the mountain, so long in labour, has been delivered of its mouse – a bright active cheery little mouse with just a touch of venom in its sharp little teeth ... You will find in your travels that this new party lifts its head all over the North. It has caught the people as I imagine the Chartist movement did. And it is of the people – such will be the secret of its success. Everywhere its bent is Socialist because Socialists are the only people who have any message for it.

> Tom Maguire to Edward Carpenter on the formation of the Independent Labour Party 1893.[1]

It was ... a cult, with affiliations in directions now quite disowned – with theosophy, arts and crafts, vegetarianism, the 'simple life' ... Morris had shed a medieval glamour over it with his stained glass *News From Nowhere*. Edward Carpenter had put it into sandals. Keir Hardie had clothed it in a cloth cap and tie. My brand of socialism was, therefore a blend or, let us say, an anthology of all these ...

> Alfred Orage on his recollection of Leeds socialism in the 1890s.[2]

Independent labour policy and the formation of the Independent Labour Party

In his history of England from 1870 to 1914, published in 1936, R. C. K. Ensor wrote that 'the ILP never became more than a socialist propaganda society'.[3] Contrast this with the observation made two years earlier by Philip Snowden, who became Labour's first Chancellor of the Exchequer: 'A National Conference of Labour and Socialist Organisations was held at Bradford in January of 1893, at which the Independent Labour Party was formed. This was the most important political event of the nineteenth century.'[4] While Snowden may well have been over-stating his case, many studies undertaken over the past twenty-five years have revealed the crucial role played by the ILP in the formation of the modern Labour Party. It was, as Laybourn describes it, from its formation in Bradford to its secession from the Labour Party in 1932, 'essentially an amalgam of provincial organisations', which provided 'the platform from which the Labour Party was launched'.[5] Soon after the formation of local organizations (in Bradford in May 1891, and in Leeds in November 1892) the national ILP was inaugurated at an historic conference in Bradford in January 1893. By 1895 there were 305 branches of the ILP nationally, one third of these in Yorkshire.

In the *Centennial History of the ILP,* published in 1992, James, Jowitt and Laybourn have comprehensively recorded and assessed what historians have revealed about the party. Together with the re-emergence of British socialist values in the 1890s, the ILP did not depend on any single source of influence (the working class or the trade unions), but on a diversity of economic, ethical and cultural factors. David Howell's *British Workers and the Independent Labour Party 1888–1906*[6] points to the contradictions in the way in which the ILP grew, in some areas flourishing despite a weak trade-union presence (as in the West Yorkshire textile districts), in other areas (for example, amongst the unorganized workers in the big cities) failing to do so. What mattered, as Bill Lancaster pointed out, were the 'culture and traditions of the locality'.[7]

In Bradford the culture and traditions were peculiarly favourable for the growth of an independent labour movement. Laybourn has shown how the party there was born in May 1891 as the Bradford Labour Union, 'conceived in the frustrations of working men' following the failure of the Manningham Mill strike, and grew to a membership of 2,000, in nineteen clubs and with two councillors by 1893. By 1906 it had its own MP (Fred Jowett in Bradford West), and between 1906 and 1914 the party held the balance of power in municipal politics.[8] The conditions that produced such successful development included, firstly, the existence of socialist groups (a branch of the Socialist League had existed since 1886); secondly, the wave of new unionism which produced a large growth in membership of the Trades Council; thirdly, the commitment and support of a small group of Nonconformist ministers who agreed with the ideas of the socialists on the causes of and remedies for poverty; but, most important of all, 'the strength and confidence of the Bradford ILP derived from its capture of the local trade union movement'.[9] Studies of Huddersfield and Halifax also identify the importance of trade-union support for the successful growth of the ILP.[10]

But while the effects of economic changes and the attitudes of trade unions were factors, they were not the only ones. In Keighley, which did not have a strong trade-union presence, the ILP also achieved some success. Here, James has shown how cultural, religious and ethical impulses were important, as people sought to redefine a sense of community in the values of socialism. Clark's study of the Colne Valley suggests that, even where trade unions were weak, the ILP was still able to thrive,[11] and that a large part of the reason for this was that ethical and moral influences behind socialism were capable of attracting groups of people searching for a *Weltanschauung* beyond the austere faces of utilitarianism and free trade on the one hand, or dogmatic socialism on the other. This was very much the case in Leeds, where the trade unions were either relatively weak in the town's main industries, or where those largely artisan trades that were organized were reluctant to embrace a socialist-led independent labour movement. Idealistic individuals from the large white-collar and middle class of Leeds, particularly its younger members, eagerly joined the new movement in the 1890s, and progressive attitudes emerging from Nonconformist religious groups provided another source of recruitment. Smith showed that, while only a minority of Nonconformists actively supported an independent labour movement, those who did so were individuals who rejected orthodox views of sinful human nature in favour of a modernist theology, which saw socialism as applied Christianity and which equated the kingdom of God as a 'this-worldly just social order'.[12] This was very much the perspective of those who formed and joined the Labour Churches which flourished in the 1890s. Jowitt has shown how religion also energized the new movement in the West Riding, which was one of the great bastions of Nonconformity and where '[t]he chapel, church and Sunday School were as much a part of the landscape as were the mills'. Although working-class religious attendance was low, the chapel and the Sunday School were the social and recreational focus for many communities, providing for many children especially 'a common corpus of knowledge, language, imagery and values'.[13] Although there was great variation in the influence of different denominations in the various communities of the region, 'the development of the Independent Labour Party in West Yorkshire was greatly helped by recourse to religious imagery and forms'.[14] The Yorkshire ILP was, as is evident from Orage's description quoted in the epigraph to this chapter, 'a sturdy cross-bred'.[15] While its young leaders in Leeds had come into the socialist movement in the 1880s with a knowledge of Marxist theory, the moral, cultural, and ethical quality placed on it by William Morris, Edward Carpenter and Keir Hardie 'reverberated best in the hearts of a generation who had picked up their little education in Sunday school or chapel'.[16]

Morris's contribution to socialist thinking, particularly his influence in reconciling socialism and art, and his conviction that socialism required a complete re-ordering of society, has been well described by Edward Thompson, and his influence on the young socialists of Leeds has been traced in the previous chapter. Edward Carpenter (1844–1929), from a wealthy middle-class family, and a graduate of Trinity Hall Cambridge, also had an influence on young Leeds socialists like Tom Maguire and Alfred Mattison. Carpenter turned against conventional middle-class values and bought a smallholding at Millthorpe in Derbyshire, with the intention of living simply through crafts and market gardening. He became a follower of Walt Whitman and published *Towards Democracy* in the mid-1880s, a long free-verse poem in the style of Whitman's *Leaves of Grass*, the theme of which was 'that spontaneity of social and personal behaviour, the freeing of sex from a damaging morality of constraint, would create conditions in which the individual might regain a sense of personal wholeness and social community'. Carpenter was involved with the SDF, formed the Sheffield Socialist Society in 1886, and remained a prominent socialist propagandist, inspiring many with his speeches and his writings for twenty years or more from 1885. Although he was castigated for his avoidance of organized political commitment (George Bernard Shaw, referring to Carpenter's sandal-making and market gardening called him a 'Nobel Savage' and sneered at 'carpenterings and illusions') he served as confidant, adviser and prophet to many – including Maguire – and Millthorpe became a place of pilgrimage for the new socialist movement.[17] While its ability to attract trade-union support to eradicate poverty by welfare reforms and to improve working conditions by government regulation was an important element in the success of the party, especially in alliance with the unions via the LRC after 1900, the ILP nevertheless drew its support from a broader social base than the working class. The key to the success of the party and the reasons for its subsequent electoral success, were that pragmatism and policies for social reform were surrounded by a wider appeal, based on ethical, moral and idealistic aspects of socialism, which were capable of attracting a variety of social groups to a realizable vision of a just society.

It was to the concerns of trade-unionists that the Leeds socialists turned in 1889 and 1890. The *Labour Programme* published by John Mahon in 1888, justified intervention in labour and trade-union politics and defined a co-operative democracy as its objective. When trade conditions changed in the late 1880s, they were strategically well placed to act. The period between 1873 and 1896 have been described by economic historians as the years of the Great Depression, but there were fluctuations in the trade cycle even within this period. In the middle of the 1880s unemployment ran at about 10 per cent, but in rapidly improving conditions it had fallen by 1889 to around 2 per cent. The effect of this was a wave of industrial militancy throughout the country which led to the phenomenon of 'new unionism' – the organization of unions for semi-skilled and unskilled workers whose attitudes to politics were very different to those of the craft trade unions. Union membership probably doubled nationally between 1888 and 1892, and went through a sustained growth – and a second period of militancy – between 1910 and 1914, so that by 1914 about 25 per cent of the working population were in trade unions, compared with 5 per cent in the mid-1880s.[18] Nationally, the 1888 strike by women at the Bryant and May factory and the strikes of the London dockers led by Ben Tillet and the gasworkers (who, led by Will Thorne, won for themselves the eight-hour day) have attracted the attention of historians. In Leeds this new unionism spread amongst tramway workers, bricklayers' labourers, tailoresses, Jewish clothing workers, general labourers and gasworkers. The high point came with the lock-out of the gasworkers in June and July 1890, when the Liberal council attempted to revoke concessions won by the Gasworkers' and General Labourers' Union (GGLU) the previous winter. In the short struggle that followed, Leeds resembled an armed camp as blackleg workers were led into the New Wortley gasworks, headed by cavalry and followed by the Lord Mayor and magistrates.[19]

In the summer of 1890, following the gasworkers' strike, members of the Socialist League in Leeds, having modified their early purism, decided to attempt to guide the strikers towards independent labour representation and made what was the first of three attempts to launch an independent labour party in Leeds. The debate among the Socialist League members about the political implications of the strike signified a parting of the ways. Maguire, in a letter to Edward Carpenter, explained the issues involved. Plainly, there was a strong divergence of opinion about the significance of the gasworkers' strike between the parliamentarians and the anarchists in the Socialist League in Leeds. Maguire put the case of the 'political' wing:

Dear C., – I hope you will forgive me for not having answered yours sooner, and I think you will when I tell you that there has been such a rumpus raised by a few demented anarchists here – since the gas riots – that it has become impossible for us to work together any longer ... Perhaps the real issue (shorn of the cloud of bitterness and personal animosity) is which of the two courses is the wisest one to take bearing in mind the events of the gasworkers' struggle. Those of us who had to do with the gasworkers in response to the men's wishes and in accordance with our ideas of policy, considered a Labour Electoral League should be formed, and accordingly this was done. Our anarchist friends, who were conspicuous by their absence in the gas fights, joined issue with us at once, attacked not only the League but ourselves, and finally told the people that no policy should be entertained but physical force. Now, while I believe in the use of physical force when necessary I think it is midsummer madness to advocate it on the public platform, and it is unlikely, as it would be undesirable, for the people to resort to it until other means had been tried and found wanting. I admit the Labour Electoral move is not all to be desired, but it seemed the next immediate step to take in order to keep the labour unions militant, and to emphasise the conflict of the workers and the employers ... For myself, I will see the L.E.L. in working order – which I daresay will be done in a couple of weeks –

and then I will have done with it and all other blessed movements for
some time to come ...[20]

The anarchist side of the split is not directly recorded for Leeds, but it
may be safely assumed that they were following the policy advocated by
the anarchist section of the Socialist League which had become influential on the newspaper *Commonweal*. In any case, the dispute marked
the effective end of the old Socialist League in Leeds.

Of the Labour Electoral League (LEL), very little is known. It was
still in existence in the autumn of 1890 and appears to have acted as a
ginger group, independent of and separate from the Leeds Trades
Council, probably composed of GGLU members and ex-Socialist League
socialists. Its function was to pressurize the LTC to adopt a policy of
labour representation. The LTC, although it had grown rapidly through
the period 1889–90, still did not represent the newly organized unskilled
workers in the GGLU, who were standing aloof from the Council. The
only unskilled group which had decided to join the LTC was the Builders'
Labourers' Union, whose representative, J. Sweeney, was the first of the
socialists in Leeds to go into the LTC with the intention of 'raising
the devil', as Mahon had put it two years earlier. He spent the winter of
1890 maligning John Judge, William Bune and William Marston
because of their alleged inactivity in relation to the problems of unskilled
workers, and because of their attitude to the tailoresses who were on
strike at the Arthurs clothing factory.

While the socialists regarded the militant actions of tailoresses,
gasworkers, builders' labourers' and Jewish tailors as the beginnings of
a labour protest, which might be developed into a political and socialist
labour movement, the LTC wished to conciliate employers and employed.
The Chamber of Commerce approached the LTC with a proposal to
form a Conciliation Board in the spring of 1890, and by July this had
been set up, composed of twelve representatives from the Chamber of
Commerce and from the LTC.[21] The Board was to provide a voluntary
service, to be used only when both sides in a dispute requested its
assistance.

The unskilled workers, organized for the most part in the GGLU,
and formed and advised by the Socialist League members, developed
along a different path from the LTC. They declined to affiliate to it and
formed instead, in January or February 1890, a Yorkshire Labour League
(YLL) which was, in effect, the Yorkshire district branch of the GGLU.
The YLL had delegates from Hull, Sheffield, Huddersfield, Halifax,
Dewsbury, Bingley, Heckmondwike and Leeds. Its stated objectives are
of particular importance since, drawn up by Maguire, Sweeney and
Cockayne – the latter a recent convert to socialist ideas – they echoed
closely the statements made by Mahon in his Labour Programme of
1888. The objectives of the YLL were as follows:

To strengthen and consolidate the labour organisations of Yorkshire by drawing them together as frequently as possible and keeping them in constant touch with each other's doings and conditions ... [It was hoped] to make the Council a bureau of statistics respecting the state of labour and trade throughout the U.K. Thus men out of work may be drafted from congested districts to places where work can be obtained without the necessity of tramping aimlessly and despairingly in search of employment. Lastly, the Council, by federating the various sections of labour, hopes to secure unity of action, together with a standard rate of wages, over the widest workable area ...[22]

The YLL council was to meet monthly, with Sweeney and Maguire as honorary members. The YLL was clearly at odds with the LTC, accusing it of interfering with its work. The *Yorkshire Factory Times* regretted the argument between the two bodies and felt inclined to put the blame on the YLL which was concerned, in the opinion of the *Yorkshire Factory Times*, not so much with trade-unionism as with 'disseminating debatable doctrines'.[23]

Changes in this policy of standing aloof from the LTC began to appear early in 1891. The LEL, mentioned by Maguire in his letter to Carpenter, was defunct by the winter of 1890–1, and, with the arrival in Leeds in January 1891 of Mahon, the decision was made to bring the socialist GGLU into the LTC. Mahon himself applied to join the LTC but was rejected, because, it was said, he was not a worker.[24]

In the meantime, to fill the political vacuum formed by the collapse, first of the Socialist League and then of the LEL, a Fabian Society was formed in Leeds, with Alfred Mattison taking a leading role. Mahon became branch secretary of the Hunslet Engineers' Labourers' branch of the GGLU, thereby becoming eligible to sit as a delegate on the LTC. At its March 1891 meeting, the LTC found itself called upon to raise its sights from its normal preoccupations with craft restriction to grander objectives. Sweeney put a proposal: 'that this Council at once takes steps to bring about a closer union of the labouring classes by federating the various trades and labour councils of Yorkshire with the view of ultimately securing the national and international federation of the workers of all trades and industries.'[25] Although the motion was defeated, the LTC was disturbed by the appearance of these politically motivated socialists at the head of a growing section of the labour movement. In a move to reduce the increasing influence of men like Sweeney, Mahon and Maguire, John Judge had, at the June meeting of the LTC, attempted to amend the council's Rule 3, to exclude 'professional agitators': 'Delegates must obtain their living from the trade and labour or the trade and labour association they represent on the Council.' The motion was defeated, but the rule was formulated vaguely enough to leave room for argument about its interpretation, and this was to remain a source of potential conflict.[26]

In their effort to ward off socialist attempts to control the politics of organized labour, the LTC leaders were given no help by the attitudes and actions of the Liberal council. An explosion of anger erupted against the latter at the July 1891 meeting of the LTC when it became known that only the old radical, Alderman Spark, had voted in favour of a motion at the Leeds town council meeting to restrict the placing of corporation contracts to businesses which paid fair wages. The normally placid LTC was enraged and, according to the *Yorkshire Factory Times*, the members present at the July monthly meeting 'practically chucked allegiance to the Liberal and Tory Parties and avowed themselves labour men'. This was almost certainly an exaggeration, but there was no doubt that the LTC became far more strident in its desire for direct labour representation, particularly at municipal level. The first reaction to the town council's contempt for the trade unions' advocacy of fair contracts was one of renewed lobbying with the Liberal Party. For example, it was decided that a group of trade-unionists should attend the next meeting of the Holbeck Liberal Association to push through a resolution condemning those who voted against placing contracts with fair houses. At the same time the gasworkers' LTC delegates began a campaign to support a proposal, initially introduced by the delegates of the National Union of Boot and Shoe Operatives (NUBSO), to the effect that the LTC should take steps to bring forward a labour candidate at the forthcoming general election. The LTC, however, took the initiative in developing a policy to secure the adoption of labour candidates for the municipal elections, since it was found that a considerable number of councillors and candidates did not, despite additional lobbying, approve of a 'fair contracts' policy. At a special meeting of the LTC lifelong Liberals and the minority of lifelong Tories, were apparently prepared 'to renounce politics altogether' and to declare for direct labour representation (for example, Henry Maundrill of the Miners' Union and John Wescoe of NUBSO). A resolution was passed expressing the opinion that 'the workers of Leeds ought to be directly represented on the borough council and that suitable means be at once adopted to obtain funds to fight a number of seats next November'. In effect, the meeting was a warning to, rather than a renunciation of, the Liberal Party. Bune, Judge and Marston, the leading figures on the LTC urged that 'the wisest plan was to take advantage of existing political organizations and try where they could to get working men candidates adopted. Unless they did that he was afraid they would be unable to get independent labour candidates.'[27]

An election committee of the LTC was set up and it was decided to oppose candidates in those wards where the party representatives were hostile to trade-unionism or fair contracts. It was decided to seek labour representation in the Holbeck, West Hunslet, and North Wards, as a result of which the meeting of the West Hunslet Liberals refused to accept the candidature of Bune, who was a member both of the LTC and the West Hunslet Liberal Association.

Snubbed by the Liberals over labour representation, the labour movement in Leeds gave an impressive show of unity in September 1891, when a special demonstration was called in support of the municipal electoral policy of the LTC. The Leeds trade-union movement witnessed the unique spectacle of old Liberal trade-unionists and new union socialists sharing the same platform: John Judge, William Bune, and William Marston, speaking with Tom Mann, Ben Tillett, Will Thorne, and the local leaders of the GGLU. Again, however, the Liberals took little notice of the warnings from the LTC leaders. Judge withdrew his candidature for the North Ward because the Liberal candidate had accepted the LTC programme. However, when Bune, who was Secretary of the Hunslet Liberal Club, withdrew his candidature for West Hunslet because his own party did not accept him, John Childerson replaced him in an attempt to force the Liberals to adopt labour candidates. In Holbeck John Leach, the LTC nominee for that ward, president of the Leeds Industrial Co-operative Society, and a Liberal Party member for twenty-five years, was angered when his candidature was not accepted by the Holbeck Liberals. Henry Maundrill then stood in his place, since Leach was not, despite his anger, prepared to act against his party. In addition to these three LTC nominees, William Cockayne of the GGLU was put up to stand for East Hunslet.

All three candidates were defeated at the municipal elections, although Cockayne and Childerson in East Hunslet and West Hunslet respectively, came close to their Liberal opponents. Following these defeats, it appears that the LTC was prepared to let the matter rest, and to hope that the Liberal Party had got the message. The LTC executive, which contained no candidates from the new unions which supported independent labour representatives, pulled in its horns and returned to the traditional practice of recommending LTC nominees to the Tory and Liberal Parties for the forthcoming School Board elections. Cockayne spoke against this action at the November 1891 LTC monthly meeting but he was overruled. Mahon, by this time an LTC delegate, issued a direct challenge to the Council by standing for the School Board elections himself. In the ensuing argument, relations between the GGLU delegates and the minority of socialists on the one hand, and the majority of trade-unionists on the other, became severely strained. At a meeting of the LTC in November, called to discuss Mahon's candidature, Marston and Judge began the proceedings by insisting that he withdrew from the meeting, since they deemed him ineligible to sit there, and Mahon was immediately defended by the GGLU delegates and by Mattison of the ASE.

In the course of the meeting the GGLU delegates withdrew – forty in all – and issued a declaration accusing the LTC of joining hands with the conventional political parties. In their absence Judge led an attack on Mahon, criticizing not only his action (against LTC policy) in contesting the School Board election, but also his 'antecedents', claiming that he was manipulating the GGLU delegates for his own personal use and that the GGLU had 'joined the Council in order to have its own way'. The superficial unity that had been displayed at the September demonstration was quickly shattered. At this point, members of the LTC who were sympathetic to the Liberal Party injected a serious complication into local labour politics. They attempted, successfully, to stir up hostility amongst the Irish labourers in the GGLU and the Builders' Labourers' Union against the GGLU leadership, and Mahon in particular, who, it was claimed, was determined to wreck the Liberal Party and consequently the hopes of Irish people for Home Rule.

The division was a real and difficult one and highlighted plainly the scale of the task involved in constructing working-class political unity. The following months were filled with bitter charges, denials and countercharges between LTC officials and the GGLU leaders; the latter were said to be too fond of whisky, stout and ale, while Judge was pressed by the GGLU to prove his charges against Mahon publicly or be thrown out of the LTC. The dispute between the two men finally came to a head at a stormy meeting of the LTC in February 1892, during which Mahon spoke for an hour, refuting the Judge's charges, including the accusation that he was interested only in preaching socialism and that he was being paid 30s. (£1.50) per week to do so as a GGLU official. Mahon claimed that he had 'as much right to preach socialism' as Judge had to preach atheism (Judge at this time was a member of the Secular Society) and felt that he had been subject to much 'unfriendliness and prejudice' from the LTC simply because he represented unskilled labourers. Judge was more astute than Mahon gave him credit for, and moved closer to the truth about the nature of his objection. Mahon, he said, 'had come in to manage the unions, with which he had no previous connection at all. He was, in fact, a born general, and not a common soldier.'[28] Nevertheless, Mahon retained the enthusiastic support of his own branch of the GGLU – the engineers' labourers – and retained his position in the LTC.

The pressure from socialists for the direct representation of labour continued. In the spring of 1892, the LTC was persuaded to accept a committee of fifteen to report on the best means of advancing labour representation. The subcommittee recommended that a 'Leeds Trades and Labour Council Electoral Union' (LEU) should be formed, a proposal which was accepted by the LTC in May 1892. It was the second attempt to form an independent labour party, the first being the short-lived LEL in 1890.

The objectives of the LEU made clear provision for independent representation (rather than through the Liberal Party) and hopes for its success were high. It was sanctioned by the LTC, and, in the words of the *Yorkshire Factory Times*, 'some of the leading spirits, for years the bulwarks of the Liberal and Tory Parties, have joined'. The LEU was to be managed by a committee of fifteen, elected annually by and from the LTC. Membership was provided for on an individual basis, at 1*s.* (5p) per annum, and the funds of the LEU and the LTC were to be kept separately. The function of the LEU was to secure the election of labour representatives to Parliament and to the town council, the School Board and the Board of Guardians. The qualifications for membership, as specified in Rule 4 of the Constitution, were somewhat ambiguous:

> That the operations of this union shall be carried on irrespective of the convenience of any political organisation. Persons holding official positions in connection with political organisations shall not be eligible for membership, and members of this union accepting official positions in any political organisation shall thereby forfeit their membership ...[29]

In the summer of 1892 the LEU began a series of public meetings in the working-class areas of Leeds, addressed by lapsed Liberals such as Henry Maundrill, John Childerson and John Judge, and socialists like Tom Maguire, John Mahon and Alfred Mattison. It was claimed that 2,000 membership cards were issued by June 1892. The support of the trade-union movement in Leeds for the new LEU can be gauged from the amount of funds that they were prepared to contribute. By August 1892 only ten of the sixty-seven trade-union branches affiliated to the LTC had donated money to the LEU fund to run municipal candidates. As a result, the LEU progressed slowly, but in September it opened its first ward club in East Hunslet, with Mattison as its secretary. At the same time, the organization had its eye on the forthcoming general election, apparently going so far as to approach Tom Mann and Sidney Webb to stand as Labour candidates in Leeds, both of whom declined. When Lawson Walton was selected as the Liberal candidate for South Leeds, the LEU members expressed annoyance, since they had hoped, surely unrealistically, that the Liberal Party would allow their labour representative a free run.

There was, in fact, a battle taking place to control the direction of the new organization. Judge, Marston, and the Lib–Labs saw the LEU as radicalizing the Liberal party. Mahon and the socialists had entirely different ambitions, however, seeing the LEU as a means of creating a new independent labour party and as a device for splitting the Liberal Party. In the middle of September the LEU brought forward G. Solley of the General Railway Workers' Union to contest South Leeds. However, he was barely two weeks into his campaign when the Lib–Lab sentiment of the LTC asserted itself. An LTC subcommittee proposed changes to the original LEU constitution, amongst which was its insistence that, while the LEU was open to all workers as individual members, the LTC should have the power to appoint two-thirds of the management committee, and also reserve a power of veto over LEU decisions. It exercised this power of veto when it reversed the decision to contest South Leeds.

The socialists of the LEU decided not to let the matter rest, and Mahon came forward in place of Solley to fight the seat. The reaction of the Liberal Party and its supporters to Mahon's candidature was violent and extreme. His first meeting at Hunslet Mechanics' Institute with Maguire and H. H. Champion on the platform, was packed with an aggressive crowd sporting the Liberal candidate's colours, which shouted down Mahon and his supporters on the platform. Then 'a determined rush was made for the platform headed by a local politician and member of the Trades Council'.[30] According to Mahon, the opposition to his candidature came chiefly from Irish Home Rulers excited to rowdyism by the speeches of Lawson Walton, the Liberal candidate. It is clear that Mahon did not suddenly decide to contest the election himself, but, rather, wished to follow through the work of the LEU and not allow that organization to die a quiet death. Shortly afterwards, Mahon had to withdraw from the contest because of a technical fault in his nomination papers. The episode aroused bitter feelings among members of the labour movement in Leeds, further alienating the small group of political socialists from the LTC, which, at its monthly meeting in September confirmed the decision not to contest South Leeds. The incident also left the socialists themselves weakened and divided: the GGLU gasworkers' branch, hitherto the spearhead of socialist initiatives but, with the worsening economic conditions prevailing from late 1892, more concerned with its survival as a trade union, disassociated itself from Mahon's candidature, passing a resolution that publicly reproached him for his 'recent political conduct, it having a tendency to injure our branch in the estimation of the public, as we believe many people erroneously thought that he was supported by this branch'.[31]

Once again a furious dispute broke out in the LTC about the reasons for Mahon's involvement in Leeds trade-unionism. Despite the rebuke from the gasworkers' branch of the GGLU, the leading political socialists – Cockayne, Mahon and Tom Paylor – were all re-elected onto the district executive committee of the GGLU. However, the hostility to Mahon in the LTC did not die down. James Sweeney, a one-time comrade of Mahon, switched sides and was responsible for inciting Irish trade-unionists in the Builders' Labourers' Union against both independent labour politics and the GGLU, seen to be amongst its main promoters. Sweeney publicly accused Mahon of stealing money from a fund set up to support the wife of the anarchist Charles Mowbray, a charge which was dropped when Mahon undertook legal action. The strain told, and shortly before Christmas 1892 Mahon resigned his post as financial secretary of the Leeds District GGLU. He went on a brief holiday and then returned to Leeds to play a crucial but controversial role in the formation and direction of the third and, in the event, enduring attempt to create an independent labour party. The old LEU was quietly buried as a result of the lack of interest from the LTC, and Maguire and Mahon steered its membership away from that organization. Together with Mattison, they transformed the old premises of the LEU in East Hunslet into the clubrooms of the new East Hunslet Independent Labour Party, sidestepping the LTC. They had no great institutional backing, although the GGLU did in fact continue to support them. At the same time, independent labour clubs were set up, with help from George Burniston, Robinson Walker of the GGLU dyers' branch, Kendall, Mahon, Marles, Mattison, Paylor, Pennington and Sylvester, in West Ward, and, in November, at Bramley. They were all trade-unionists, but only the GGLU representatives had the official support of their union. Early in October, Mahon and Maguire were placed on a committee to work out a new set of rules and a constitution for what was to become the Leeds Independent Labour Party.[32] Within a span of twenty years this party was to transform local politics and formed part of a process which, over a longer period, destroyed the Liberal Party.

By January 1893 the Leeds ILP consisted of seven ward-based independent labour clubs (Armley Clarion; Armley Labour; Bramley; North East Ward; Holbeck; East Hunslet; and West Ward).[33] It had already formulated its own objectives before the Bradford conference in January 1893 when the national ILP was formed. The remarkable feature of the objectives of the Leeds ILP in January 1893 is that, although the organization was the direct creation of those socialists who had pioneered socialism in Leeds, and indeed in much of Yorkshire, no mention was made in the programme of the word 'socialist'. The objectives of the new party were simply stated:

To obtain Independent Labour representatives on legislative and administrative bodies, in order to promote improvement in social conditions and in the administration of public affairs. To exercise the independent use of the Labour vote, in contests where no Independent Labour candidates are nominated, in such manner as will best further the programme and policy of the independent Labour Party. To formulate a programme of practical measures for the redress of labour grievances, and to determine on the political policy for the realization of such programme.[34]

The ILP had got rid of the troublesome and ambiguous Rule 4 that had dogged the LEU, which had stated that only officials of other political parties were barred from membership. This had allowed the Lib–Labs to keep a foot in both camps, with the stronger foot in the Liberal Party. It was now plainly laid down that members of the ILP could not belong to any other political party. The constitution was a democratic one, with a large amount of power vested in the ILP ward clubs, each of which was entitled to provide four delegates to the Leeds ILP Central (and later Federal) Council. The power to determine the general policy of the party was vested in the Central Council, both in terms of the election manifestoes and long-term policy directions, but each club had the power to recall its delegates. The ward clubs were also responsible for the selection of municipal candidates, while joint meetings of ward clubs forming a parliamentary constituency were entitled to select a parliamentary candidate. The Executive Committee formed by the Central Council was to have administrative functions only. This democratic constitution was somewhat mitigated by the arrangements that determined the distribution of finance for local and parliamentary elections, since the Central Council had full power to allocate resources.

The politics of the ILP under the influence of Maguire and Mahon

In seeking to understand the nature of the ILP and of the early Labour Party, the problems confronted by those involved in setting up both organizations must be clarified. Edward Thompson, in his authoritative pioneering study of Yorkshire and Leeds labour history, has written that the essence of the ILP was its socialism.[35]

But there are difficulties in this analysis. Maguire and Mahon, soon after the Leeds ILP had been formed, seemed, paradoxically, to be playing down the socialist rhetoric of the new organization, and for long periods up to 1914, socialist politics failed to gain the support that the euphoric years of the early 1890s suggested they might. Indeed, the revolutionary socialists of the 1880s had apparently undergone a conspicuous transition in their political strategy. Looking back on this period, Mattison later recalled:

> Up to 1890 the Leeds Party had been quite revolutionaries, and had seen no hope whatever in Parliament. Between 1890 and 1893 came a change in outlook: They began to see the need and the possibility of political action, and while industrial organisation was being carried out a political programme was being designed.[36]

At the foundation conference of the national ILP in Bradford on 13 and 14 January 1893, the Leeds delegates attempted to persuade the conference to reject an explicit commitment to socialism. When it was moved 'That the object of the Independent Labour Party shall be to secure the collective and communal ownership of all the means of production, distribution and exchange', Mahon rose to suggest an amendment which expressed the policy that the party had already adopted in Leeds: 'That the objects of the Independent Labour Party shall be to secure the separate representation and protection of labour interests on public bodies'.[37] This amendment was supported by the Leeds delegates, A. Marles of the Leeds Fabian Society, and William Vickers of the ASE, a recent convert to the ILP group in Leeds and the first chairman of the Leeds ILP Central Council. It was lost by 91 votes to 16.[38]

Edward Thompson put the slow development of a socialist movement in Leeds down to the structural features of the Leeds economy, as well as to a more subjective cause – that is, the failure of socialist leadership locally. Maguire, because of a personal reticence and the debilitating effects of an illness which was soon to kill him, allowed Mahon – 'vain, incurably quarrelsome, and given to intrigue' – to assume the leadership of the movement.[39] The observation may be contrasted to the situation in Bradford, where the generation of socialists which entered the movement in the mid-1880s largely survived to guide it to its successes up to 1914. There is a good deal of truth in this explanation. Mahon was quarrelsome and difficult; he had exasperated William Morris and infuriated the LTC leaders. The manner of his leaving the Socialist League and contributing to its eventual break-up has been criticized by Thompson as involving unnecessary deception, instead of openly debating the issue of reform versus revolution. When Engels declined to finance his attempts to build up provincial socialist groups committed to a transitional political programme, Mahon became increasingly dependent on H. H. Champion, whose own view of labour politics was highly opportunistic. Champion had earlier been the secretary of the Social Democratic Federation but he had not joined Morris, Mahon and the others when they broke away to form the Socialist League. In 1887 Champion led an initiative for a new practical political party and broke with the SDF, going on to work with the Labour Electoral Committee formed by the TUC in 1886. He became metropolitan organizer of the Labour Electoral Association, as the LEC had become known. With his own financial resources, his policy was simply to follow the example of the Irish Party in Parliament and make the labour vote count. He and his group of followers intervened at a number of by-elections in 1888 and began to publish the *Labour Elector*, advocating practical reform measures like the eight-hour day.[40]

In August 1892 Mahon wrote to Champion about the vacancy in South Leeds, implying that Champion might finance him in a contest; the money was forthcoming. From this point on, Champion appears to have regarded Mahon as one of his 'Lieutenants' in his bid to capture the 1893 ILP conference in Bradford in order to be able to force a pragmatic political line on it:

I mean to have as Lieutenants men who won't scuttle at the first shot
and who will agree with me that our only chance is to go for the Liberals all along the line, without gloves. It is possible … to put out 50
Liberals at the next election by running men in 10 seats and voting
Tory in the other 40 (this will make the ILP what the Irish Party has
been made by similar tactics – a national, not a local, organization).[41]

Champion's policy at the South Leeds by-election in 1892 was not to
gain a platform for socialist ideas, nor even to win the seat, but to 'spoil
Walton's [the Liberal candidate] chances'. He even promised Mahon
that he would raise enough money at the general election to enable the
Leeds ILP to fight all three divisions held by the Liberal Party, 'especially if the Liberals and Irish are insolent'.[42] Champion was evidently
pleased with his 'Lieutenant' even though Mahon did not actually go
to the poll. However, he put pressure on Mahon to go for 'practical
programmes' and not for socialism, and to attempt to get as many 'Cham-
pionites' as possible at the 1893 ILP foundation conference to force
through the same ideas:

The history of the Irish movement shows that the only way to get
popular support is to prove that the man who pays 3d. to the
movement gets 1/- out of it (like the bunch of carrots before the
donkey). So I say that donkey the British workman wants relief from
the immediate evil he feels … [which Champion specified as irreg-
ularity of employment, low pay, the workhouse, and pauperism through
accidents at work] The remedies, sound on Socialist theories and
quite easily realized, are, for 1 and 2, eight hours, and trade unionism;
for 3, pensions; for 4, employers liability … Think it out. Then set
one attitude to the enemy. I will quarrel when that programme is
carried out, not before.[43]

It is not possible to say how much this private correspondence
influenced the Leeds ILP as a branch, but it did influence Mahon who,
at the conference, took up a Championite position and was supported by
two of the Leeds delegates including the party chairman. Mahon lost
the amendment that he put forward (advocating labour representation
rather than socialism as the objective of the ILP), and he does not
appear to have been in touch with Champion after the conference. In
Leeds his position went from bad to worse, since he was beginning to
make enemies, even among the socialists. In the winter of 1893 he was
expelled from the Leeds ILP. The reason was that the local socialists
suspected that national intrigue and interference were imposing too
heavily on local affairs. Some of the Leeds socialists had already suspected that Champion was interfering with the Leeds movement, with
Mahon as his mouthpiece in the South Leeds election, and feelings of

mistrust and bitterness were undoubtedly building up. These exploded into open hostility following Mahon's behaviour over the candidature of John Lister in the Halifax by-election in February 1893. Lister was the owner of the Shibden Hall estate in Halifax and the first treasurer of the national ILP. During the course of that election – among the first to be fought officially by the new nationally constituted ILP – Mahon took it upon himself to attack Lister in the Halifax press because, he claimed, during the campaign he 'saw Lister gradually sever his connection with ILP policy as laid down at Bradford ... Lister was pledged to the Newcastle programme, but never a word did he say about the ILP policy'.[44]

On 16 February, the Leeds ILP Central Council met to consider these events. A proposal to suspend Mahon was carried by 23 votes to 8. In entering into one too many such actions Mahon had become isolated, and a victim of his own intrigue. He seems to have felt that, although an independent labour party had been formed in Leeds it had little idea of policy or organization, and that, particularly given the quiescence of Maguire in 1893, it was lacking in leadership. The fault was not wholly on his side. Still a young man, in his early thirties when the ILP was formed, he had experienced a great deal in the socialist movement and had learned a lot through it. He was a fine public speaker and a combative debater, hard to cross in argument. These attributes, particularly valuable in a tramping propagandist addressing outdoor public meetings, were of less value in the small decision-making meetings of the ILP ward clubs and Central Council, where men much newer to the movement than Mahon nevertheless had an equal right to speak, and to see that collective decisions were made binding.

The fact that the 'modern' phase of socialism was beginning, bringing problems of party discipline and of applying the vision electorally, presented difficulty for the old outdoor pioneers. In 1893 the Leeds ILP was lacking in experience and was riddled with rivalries and jealousies. Six months after its formation it had 400 names registered – 'the worst grade of the labouring classes – I should say the majority of them are men who live in lodgings houses', according to William Vickers. Thus, although the ILP had made some progress among the unemployed, it had made little amongst the trade unions. It still had much to do in unifying itself and had a long way to go before it gained widespread support.

A strong lead on policy was required. Vickers did not think that Maguire would provide it because he had 'a slight natural bias towards indolence' and only on occasions during the campaigns of the unemployed had he asserted himself. Maguire was feeling the effects of a decade of campaigning. Despite his early and lone advocacy of socialist ideas in Leeds in 1883 and 1884, he did not like the role of leadership in an organization, although his imagination was fired by outdoor propaganda meetings. Part of the reason for his refusal to move to London to join the leaders of the Socialist League in 1885 was the feeling that, in the exalted company of William Morris and the rest, he might not be up to the task. Similarly, he was pleased to be able to relinquish the secretaryship of the Leeds Socialist League in 1886–1887 to Tom Paylor, and he had confided to Edward Carpenter after the formation of the LEL in 1890 that he would retire from it 'and all other blessed movements for some time to come. I'll retire into a corner and write poetry and revenge myself on mankind in that way.'[45]

Carpenter's description of Maguire is worth extensive quotation, because it sheds light on the character of the man:

Though genial and sociable, there was about him a certain reserve and aloofness, which I believe most of his friends felt. And yet it was not difficult to see that his life was really rather lonely, and wanting in elements which are more or less necessary to everyone; not difficult to see that he suffered. Of the weakness of habit that grew upon him in later years, and which was largely, no doubt, the result of his life conditions, he was acutely conscious; yet, for reasons which are only too easy to understand, he would never lift himself out of it. The mental and physical depression of large town life, the want of true sociability anywhere, the void of personal affection trying delusively to fill itself by the conviviality of the cup, the need which artistic and sensitive natures often experience under modern conditions, the need of forgetting the hideous monotony of their surroundings – all these things were to Tom Maguire, as they were to so many others, the kind of Hydra with which in his inner nature he had to battle – even as outwardly he was fighting with its counterpart in society at large.[46]

There is no doubt also that he had considerable charisma as a speaker, a factor which was important in the recruitment of many of the early socialist converts. As Alfred Mattison recalled:

My first meeting with Tom Maguire was also the occasion of my first acquaintance with socialism. It must have been sometime early in 1886 that, strolling through the Market-place of Leeds, my attention was attracted to a pale but pleasant featured young man, who in a clear voice was speaking to a motley crowd. After listening for a while I began to feel a strange sympathy with his remarks, and – what is more – a sudden interest in and liking for the speaker; and I remember how impatiently I waited for his reappearance on the following Sunday. A few months later, and I joined 'the feeble band, the few' and became a member of the Leeds branch of the Socialist League ...[47]

The last years of Maguire's life were spent in continued reflection on the relationship between labour and socialist politics. He wrote regularly for the *Yorkshire Factory Times* and the *Labour Leader*, the new national newspaper of the ILP. In Leeds, he also wrote for *The Labour Chronicle*, a newspaper started by Mattison and J. Brotherton (the latter a member of the ASE and active in Leeds socialist politics from 1893, joining the ILP through his participation in the unemployment campaign of 1893–4). For two months, in October and November 1893, he was the editor of a second and equally short-lived ILP newspaper, the *Labour Champion*. There had been an earlier newspaper, *The Workman*, which appeared in 1890 to advocate the extension of union organization amongst the unskilled. By 1893 Maguire had become disappointed and sceptical. He suspected the motivation of many of the individuals who were joining the ILP, perhaps as a route to a political career:

> People call themselves socialists ... but what they really are is just ordinary men with socialist opinions hung round, they haven't got it inside of them ... Taking them for all in all, they were a nation of beggarly clods ... rich and poor alike aiming at the ideal state of existence enjoyed by the stalled ox. And it was to those people that the idealists came and said 'Cast away your cares and sorrows: behold, we will pass a resolution to nationalize things in general, and the bands will play away poverty while we go walking in shady lanes ... They spoke of great eternal principles, and called upon the people not to lose sight of what they were unable to see; they pictured in beautiful colours the society of the future when the inspiring motive was to be 'each for all and all for each'. But the people laughed incredulously, expressing their doubts ... For the people knew themselves better than the idealists knew them. These fellows, they said, take us for a lot of heroes and martyrs, but we know what we are – a mean spirited, mixed crowd of miserable devils, with not the courage to call our souls our own. What's the use of saying we can do without masters when we can't ...[48]

The mood of the people that Maguire had sensed did not encompass a desire for dramatic or rapid social change. The ILP could not expect to make converts beyond a small minority of enlightened individuals. The most active members of the trade-union movement at local branch level were joining the Leeds branch of the party – Walter Wood, Tom Paylor, John Brotherton, C. S. Lucas, William Vickers, Robinson Walker, J. E. Smith, etc. There was also a clear trend towards the recruitment of people outside the manual working class: 'Sentimental clerks and light labourers in the warehouses of commercialism ... A few middle class people, and occasionally a stray Bohemian lent colour and good temper to the proceedings.' The immediate line of policy for such a party lay in agitation on behalf of whatever discontents the working-class community expressed; the principal one for the 1890s was to be unemployment. By this method it was anticipated that the ILP might gradually gain credibility, and 'gather in almost all the existing groups troubled with a grievance'. Only this piecemeal step-by-step approach was workable, according to Maguire. In 1893 he still believed that there would be in the future something in the nature of a dramatic transition to socialism, but he now regarded the nature of that event as something of a mystery.[49]

It might appear from this account of Maguire's ideas in the years immediately before he died that what he brought into the ILP at its formation in Leeds was merely a watered-down Fabianism.[50] There is some truth in this. There had been a pragmatic adjustment to the realities of politics, an acceptance of the need for a form of welfare state. However, there were important differences. Maguire and Mahon had both, by 1893, placed the campaign for parliamentary and municipal social reform at the centre of their political activities; but this was to be a phase of activity grounded both in socialism, defined as democratic control of industrial and political institutions, and in the concept of class struggle.[51] The priority was to tackle the obstacles to unity. These were seen as poverty and unemployment in the economic sphere; and the political fragmentation of the working class, caused by the domination of the Liberal Party over a large part of the working-class electorate. The immediate object of ILP policy became the harrying of the Liberal Party locally in an attempt to bring about its destruction – the wards selected for attack were all Liberal Party strongholds. At the same time, a realistic assessment of ILP weakness at the elections was made. Much had to be learned about the details of election organization. Two ILP candidates were run in 1893 and the results were disappointing.

The international spread of capital following upon the technical change and the increased productivity of labour resulted in unemployment at home, compounded by increased competition from abroad. To Maguire, the solution lay neither in succumbing to the growing demand for protectionist policies nor in a continued defence of free-trade policies. It was important for the ILP to have a programme presenting its own distinctive practical solutions to real problems. In Leeds Maguire had worked towards the idea of the restriction of production by the device of the legally enacted eight-hour day, the consequent strengthening of trade-unionism, and the expansion of home demand by increasing purchasing power. For more specific crises involving unemployment in particular trades, Maguire argued that the potential existed for a more dramatic transformation of production relationships: 'Given a fair, liberal start, such a scheme as the one advanced by J. L. Mahon, some four or five years ago, in his interesting little book *A Labour Programme*, seems to have "practical" writ large on the face of it.'[52]

Two years after the formation of the ILP in Leeds, the two people who had had most influence in the process that led to its formation had disappeared from the movement. Tom Maguire died on 8 March 1895, and his importance to the political development of the labour movement in Leeds was widely acknowledged. He received an obituary notice in the *Labour Leader* from Keir Hardie, and more detailed appraisals appeared in the *Labour Leader* by A. T. Marles and in the *Yorkshire Factory Times* by Ben Turner. Marles wrote: 'He was the father of socialism in Yorkshire. Other men may have worked as long for the cause, but they themselves would be the first to admit that no man amongst them ever exerted the same influence, or had such power of organization as Maguire had.'[53] He was remembered by trade-unionists as the major personality in the formation of the unions of the unskilled, including the Builders' Labourers' Union and the GGLU in 1889–90, and the leader of the gasworkers' strike of 1890. Other branches of the GGLU, including those of the dyers, clayworkers, paviours, engineers' labourers and others, were formed by him, and he also worked with Isabella Ford – a suffragist and early ILP propagandist – in the organization of the Tailoresses' Union in 1888–89.[54]

Maguire's funeral took place at Burmantofts Cemetery after 400 people had marched in procession from Maguire's home in Lincoln's Field Terrace in the east of the town. Representatives of labour organizations throughout Yorkshire attended the funeral:

> At the graveside the coffin was lowered into the earth, and the religious ceremony being dispensed with, Duncan, of the Labour Church and the Shop Assistants Union, gave a good and feeling address. This was followed by a reading of William Morris's 'John Ball', tenderly read by Alf Mattison, and Maguire's personal friend, J. L. Mahon, closed the ceremony by another address, delivered with firmness and feeling.[55]

Recapitulating, it may be seen that socialist politics had a complicated and difficult birth in Leeds in the 1880s. A small group of pioneers, led by Maguire and Mahon, began to develop a conception of politics incompatible with the outlooks of the Tory and Liberal Parties. In the summer of 1890 the first independent political organization of labour was formed. When this collapsed the attempt was then made early in 1892 to force the LTC to support independent labour politics. Determined opposition from Lib–Labs killed this organization and the third attempt had to be made outside the LTC, outside, that is, the major labour organization in the town. This third attempt, culminating in 1892–3 in the Independent Labour Party, still had to influence the labour movement. Strategic guidance for the ILP was elaborated by Maguire and Mahon, but these ideas were not fully absorbed or understood by the party as it struggled for support and recognition in the 1890s.

Notes

1.   Isabella Ford (ed.), *Tom Maguire, A Remembrance* (Manchester, 1895).
2.   Quoted in P. Mairet, *A. R. Orage: A Memoir* (London, 1936), pp. 40–1.
3.   R. C. K. Ensor, *England 1870–1914* (Oxford, 1936), pp. 265–6.
4.   P. Snowden, *An Autobiography* (London, 1934), p. 53, quoted in D. James, T. Jowitt and K. Laybourn (eds), *The Centennial History of the Independent Labour Party* (Halifax, 1992).
5.   K. Laybourn, 'Recent Writing on the History of the ILP 1983–1932', in James, Jowitt and Laybourn (eds), *The Centennial History*, p. 317.
6.   David Howell, *British Workers and the Independent Labour Party 1888–1906* (Manchester, 1983).
7.   James, Jowitt and Laybourn (eds), *The Centennial History*, p. 326.
8.   K. Laybourn, 'The Bradford ILP and Trade Unionism', in James, Jowitt and Laybourn (eds), *The Centennial History*, pp. 137–8.
9.   *Ibid.*, p. 146.
10. P. Dawson, 'The Halifax Independent Labour Movement: Labour and Liberalism': and R. Perks, 'The Rising Sun of Socialism: Trade Unionism and the Emergence of the Independent Labour Party in Huddersfield', both cited in James, Jowitt and Laybourn (eds), *The Centennial History*, p. 321.
11. D. Clark, *Colne Valley: Radicalism to socialism; the portrait of a northern constituency in the formative years of the Labour Party 1890–1910* (London, 1981).
12. L. Smith, *Religion and the Rise of Socialism* (Keele, 1993), p. 167.
13. T. Jowitt, 'Religion and the Independent Labour Party', in K. Laybourn and D. James (eds), *The Rising Sun of Socialism: The Independent Labour Party in the Textile District of the West Riding of Yorkshire between 1890 and 1914* (West Yorkshire Archive Service, 1991), pp. 124–5.
14. *Ibid.*, p. 131.
15. The phrase is Edward Thompson's, in 'Homage to Tom Maguire', in A. Briggs and J. Saville (eds), *Essays in Labour History* (London, 1967), p. 290.
16. *Ibid.*, p. 291.
17. J. Saville and J. Bellamy (eds), *Dictionary of Labour Biography* 2 (Basingstoke, 1974), pp. 85–92.
18. E. H. Hunt, *British Labour History 1815–1914* (London, 1981).
19. For a good account, see Thompson, 'Homage To Tom Maguire', pp. 293–300.
20. Maguire to Carpenter, 30 July 1890, quoted in Ford (ed.), *Tom Maguire*, p. ix.
21. *Yorkshire Factory Times (YFT)*, 4 July 1890.
22. *Ibid.*, 7 February 1890.
23. *Ibid.*, 7 March 1890.
24. *Ibid.*, 20 February 1891.
25. *Ibid.*, 13 March 1891.
26. *Ibid.*, 12 June 1891.
27. *Ibid.*, 28 August 1891.
28. *Ibid.*, 26 February 1892.

29. *Ibid.*, 3 June and 1 July 1892.
30. *Ibid.*, 23 September 1892.
31. *Ibid.*, 30 September 1892.
32. *Ibid.*, 14 October 1892.
33. See ILP, Report of the first general conference (1893), where these seven branches are listed.
34. From the constitution of the Leeds ILP, in *YFT*, 13 January 1893.
35. Thompson, 'Homage to Tom Maguire', p. 311.
36. A. Mattison, *Notebook* 4, 1 February 1918 (unpublished MSS).
37. ILP, Report of first general conference (1893), p. 4.
38. *Ibid.* The 'Leeds amendment' was lost by a vote of 91 to 16.
39. Thompson, 'Homage to Tom Maguire', pp. 303–4.
40. This account of Champion's politics is based on the interpretation of H. Pelling, *Origins of the Labour Party, 1880–1900* (London, 1965), pp. 56–61.
41. Mahon–Champion correspondence, 5 September 1892.
42. Champion to Mahon, 15 September 1892.
43. Champion to Mahon, 9 October 1892.
44. *YFT*, 24 February 1893.
45. Ford (ed.), *Tom Maguire*, pp. xi–xii.
46. *Ibid.*, p. xiii. Carpenter also wrote that Maguire 'could be a little keen and satirical when thwarted or opposed – sometimes wounding even his friends in this way ...' (*ibid.*, p. xii).
47. *Ibid.*, pp. xiii–xiv.
48. Maguire, 'In The Lists: An Inquiry into The Causes of Trade Depressions, Their Growth, Development, and Remedy,' in *ibid.*, p. 115.
49. 'Bardolph' (pseudonym of Maguire), 'Looking Sideways: An Historical Sketch', *Labour Leader*, 19 December 1896.
50. See Maguire, 'Casual Remarks', *Labour Leader*, 1 September 1894. This was one of the last articles written by him. His view was that any progressive reform which addressed working-class grievances was worthwhile if *achieved independently*. It was the strengthening of the rank and file of the labour movement which he considered to be important, whether that strengthening was in political or in industrial activity: 'To the workers any gain coming indirectly and not achieved by their own organised effort is not worth the having. In order then to avoid the mistakes of the past the ILP must fall more closely into touch with the humbler wants of the people ... [and] make itself familiar with workshop conditions and workaday life. Aimless general propaganda should not be followed up Sunday after Sunday ... but after a certain local standing has been gained local abuses should be brought into prominence by means of specific agitation.' Grandiose conceptions of socialist objectives had to be avoided because '... the people don't doubt the truth and desirability of socialism; but they do doubt themselves and their ability to attain it. And this overwhelming doubt of theirs extends also to us ... The indifference of the mass really amounts to lack of confidence in themselves to do anything for themselves ... the method that sufficed to bring over these more active spirits will not fulfil necessarily for the passive unleavened mass, and it is with this problem that the ILP is at present confronted. If the ILP were a mere apostolate

whose one aim was the propagation of the principles of socialism, probably the methods pretty generally in use today would in time (if not eternity) penetrate and permeate the vast bulk of people. But that is what the ILP is not and cannot in the nature of things effectively be ...'

51. By this date the constitution of the Leeds ILP included the objective: 'The collective ownership of the land and all means of production, distribution and exchange'. *Labour Chronicle*, June 1893.

52. *YFT*, February 1893: 'Home Colonies and the Labour Policy'.

53. *Labour Leader*, 23 March 1895.

54. See also 'The Battles Maguire Fought', *YFT*, March 5 1897, and the obituary by 'Sweeper Up' (Ben Turner), *YFT*, 15 March 1895.

55. *YFT*, 15 March 1895.

Chapter 5

Building the Broad Church: Trade-Unionism, Labour Politics and Socialism, 1890–1914

Keir Hardie had prophesied since the eighties, that a living party thus acting together in parliament would focus labour aspirations in a way that no amount of theoretic propaganda could do. The future was to prove him right.

R. C. K. Ensor, *England 1870–1914*.[1]

From my home on the outskirts to the Bank in the middle of the city; from the head-office of the Bank to the branches at Armley, Beeston and Chapletown, I passed through areas in which factories were only relieved by slums ... a wilderness of stone and brick with soot falling in between. Drab and stunted wage slaves drifted through the stink and clatter ... For a year or two my way home passed through the City Square, where a political agitator sometimes drew a crowd around him; and sometimes I would stop and listen. In one way or another, this environment gradually penetrated the armour of my inherited prejudices. Ugliness and poverty, dirt and drabness, were too universal to be ignored. The questioning intelligence which was slowly awakening in me began to question the material things before my eyes. I found that other people had questioned them: not only Disraeli, but Carlyle, Ruskin and Morris; and that they were being questioned by people around me.

Herbert Read on Leeds *c*.1910.[2]

Trade unions and Labour politics

Following the pioneering activities of the 1880s and 1890s, the conditions for an effective consolidation of an independent national Labour Party were secured in the early years of the twentieth century. As large numbers of workers, who had previously retained some of the status of craft independence, began to see this threatened by the effects of

85

mechanization, they moved towards labour politics. Nationally, the crucial event in enabling this was the formation on 27 February 1900, at the Memorial Hall London, of the Labour Representation Committee (LRC). Between May 1900 and March 1904 most of the Trades Councils in West Yorkshire had become affiliated, and within a few years of the formation of the Leeds branch LRC in October 1902, most of the towns of West Yorkshire had their own local LRCs.[3]

In 1900 the new LRC returned 2 MPs, one of whom was James Keir Hardie. After the general election of 1906 this number had risen to 29 and by 1910 to 42. This disappointing performance was in part the result of the organizational immaturity of the new party which, before 1918, had relatively few permanent local organizers and agents to maximize the vote for the party. It was also the result of a franchise in which up to five million working-class males were disenfranchised because of technical difficulties in registering them.[4]

If the changing political culture that was affecting the country did not show distinctively in the form of parliamentary election results, the fundamental strength of the new labour politics appeared unequivocally at the level of local electoral politics. In 1901 Labour representatives won 26 seats on local councils throughout Yorkshire; by 1913 they held 85 municipal seats, providing the bedrock on which parliamentary success was soon to be built.[5] Having dominated West Yorkshire urban politics for much of the nineteenth century, the Liberal Party nationally declined from a seemingly unchallengeable position of having 400 MPs after the 1906 general elections, to a mere 40 in 1924, while the Labour Party, which had only a small number of MPs early in the twentieth century, had enough (191) by 1923 to form a minority government. A key feature of this change was the attachment of the trade-union movement to independent labour politics. What the research of Laybourn and others has shown nationally is that '[w]ithout a shadow of a doubt, the Labour party had secured the trade-union vote before 1914. By the beginning of 1914 trade unions with a membership of 1,207,841 had voted on the necessity of establishing political funds for the Labour party.'[6]

Locally, the work of socialists provided the vision and dedication which secured this change, while a series of conflicts in industrial disputes, often with Liberal employers, saw the new party grow steadily. Nationally, the Taff Vale judgement of 1901 – when the Taff Vale Railway Company successfully claimed damages for losses incurred in a strike against the Amalgamated Society of Railway Servants – resulted in a surge of trade-union affiliations to the LRC (from 350,000 in 1901 to 850,000 in 1903). In Leeds and Bradford, both strongly influenced by ILP leadership, the Trades Councils had affiliated to the LRC even before Taff Vale; after the judgement, those at Halifax, Wakefield, Keighley, Dewsbury and Batley, Huddersfield and Shipley followed suit.[7] The Taff Vale judgement was reversed in the Trades Disputes Act of

1906, but it was yet another legal action, paralleled by a tide of locally generated conflicts between 1909 and 1914, which fuelled the next phase of expansion. The legal action became known as the Osborne judgement, when Walter Osborne, a trade-unionist opposed to independent labour policies, succeeded in 1908 and 1909 in using the law to prevent the Amalgamated Society of Railway Servants from levying funds from its members to support the Labour Party. When in 1913 the Trade Union Act allowed trade-unionists to conduct secret ballots, 70 per cent of those who voted were in favour of funding labour representation.[8] This chapter deals with how these changes came about in Leeds. We begin by noting how changes in the organization of work and a general expansion of trade-unionism slowly undermined the security and the political assumptions of Lib–Lab trade-unionists.

The Leeds Trades Council and trade-union organization

Affiliated membership of the Leeds Trades Council doubled between 1886 and 1890, and again between 1890 and 1892. For the remainder of the 1890s growth appears to have been slow, maintaining the expansion achieved in the early part of the decade, but not significantly adding to it. A second period of advance occurred in the early years of the twentieth century, peaking in 1907, with 19,000 trade-union members affiliated to the Trades Council. All this took place against the background of a 22 per cent increase in Leeds labour force between 1881 and 1891, partly the result of a high rate of immigration. In the thirty years from 1881 the labour force grew by 54 per cent.[9]

The composition of the LTC underwent some important changes. In September 1889 the first of the new unionist organizations, the Builders' Labourers' Union, joined, beginning a series of affiliations which was to alter its occupational and political balance. In the summer of 1889 Maguire, Mattison, Paylor and other members of the Socialist League assisted Will Thorne in the formation of a Leeds branch of the Gas-workers' and General Labourers' Union for the men at the New Wortley and Meadow Lane gasworks. By the end of the 1890s the GGLU in Leeds had formed thirty-four branches, covering a membership of over 6,000, including gas-stokers, yard men, coal-wheelers, carters, dyers, engineers' labourers, plumbers' labourers and general labourers. A large part of the growth in trade-unionism in the early 1890s was the result of the growth of the GGLU and of unskilled and semi-skilled unionism (see Table 5).

In 1892 the ASE was the largest single trade union, with 36 delegates on the LTC, while the GGLU ranked equal second with the Leeds branch of the NUBSO, with 22 delegates. By 1904 these positions had been reversed; the GGLU had by far the largest delegation with 42 representatives, while the ASE had dropped to 24 and the NUBSO to 20. A milestone was reached when, in 1900, Walter Wood, GGLU district president, was also voted in as president of the LTC, the first official of an unskilled or semi-skilled trade union in Leeds to achieve the position. Nevertheless, the emergence of support for independent labour politics was not simply the result of the capture of the movement by the GGLU. Significant changes were also occurring which affected the status, security and, ultimately, the political attitudes of the established trades, and these changes are outlined below.

Table 5   The growth of the Trades Council, 1883–1910

Year	Total no. of trade unions	Total nos. affiliated
1883	–	2,450*
1886	–	2,500*
1890	–	5,600*
1891	–	10,000*
1892	46	11,400*
1894	55	12,490
1895	58	12,500
1896	55	13,068
1897	57	13,850
1898	58	12,500
1904	–	17,000
1906	–	15,000
1907	–	19,000
1908	–	16,800
1909	–	17,600
1910	67	18,200

* = Estimate.

Sources: Comparative Statistical Tables, All Trade Unions, PP (1899), XCII, p. 261. Board of Trade, Report on Trade Unions, 1908–1910, PP (1912–13), XLVII. Trades Council, Annual Reports. *Yorkshire Factory Times.*

The impact of general trade-unionism had a further effect on the LTC in that its horizons were broadened to take in other forms of organization. In February 1893 a conference was held in Leeds to propose a scheme for a regional federation of existing Trades Councils, and by the summer of 1893 such an organization had come into existence, composed of representatives from thirteen Yorkshire centres (Leeds, Bradford, Huddersfield, Castleford, Spen Valley, Wakefield, Doncaster,

Mexborough, Brighouse, Morley, Shipley, York and Dewsbury). By 1894 the Yorkshire Federation of Trades Councils (YFTC) represented 52,000 trade-unionists in the region. Ben Turner of the General Union of Weavers and Textile Workers was its first secretary.[10] The YFTC saw its function as the co-ordinator of normal Trades Council activities, so that these could be expressed more effectively at county and parlia-mentary levels. Significantly, the need for such a federation was justified because 'capital is rearing up huge syndicates, trusts, and combines and these are generally without soul or conscience. Labour must be pre-pared for any assault made on its rights …'[11] Pressure to develop and broaden forms of organization to defend the rights of organized labour was mounting through the 1890s. Challenges to the power, role and status of skilled workers in the main Leeds industries together with a general insecurity caused by a new phase of mechanization were to result in the emergence of widespread trade-union support for independent labour politics. The reasons for this can be well illustrated by a consideration of the experiences of industrial relations in the main Leeds industries.

The engineering industry and the Amalgamated Society of Engineers

In Yorkshire as a whole the ASE had a total membership of 10,080, which comprised approximately one-eighth of the national membership of the union in 1897.[12] While the ASE was one of the three largest trade unions in Leeds, and the Leeds membership rate was the largest in York-shire, the observation was consistently made that the engineering industry in Leeds was still very badly organized. It was calculated that of the 18,000 workmen in the trade and eligible to join, only 2,000 were ASE members in 1889 (see Table 6). The result was that rates of pay and the quality of working conditions also lagged behind. In January 1890, for

Table 6   ASE membership in Leeds, 1851–1900

	No. of branches	Total membership
1851	2	583
1860	4	858
1868	5	1,274
1892	11	2,215
1897	11	2,631
1900	11	2,483

Source: Trades Council Reports, and *Yorkshire Factory Times*.

example, the *Yorkshire Factory Times* claimed that the average weekly rate in Leeds, at 28*s*. (£1.40) per week, was at least 6*s*. (30p) behind the rate in Sheffield. In addition to lower wages, Leeds engineering was also said to be backward in terms of long hours worked in the form of overtime, which was, according to the ASE, 'a greater evil in Leeds than any other town in the U.K'.[13]

The state of industrial relations was revealed in some detail in the evidence of an engineering employer to the Royal Commission on Labour in 1892. Reginald Wigram of John Fowler and Co. Ltd., Leeds Engineers, pointed out that labour relations in the Leeds industry were different from other areas, and he cited the situation in the North East and Tyneside, where collective bargaining and arbitration machinery were well developed and where trade-unions' and employers' associations were well organized. Leeds engineering employers had a strong and established preference not to deal with trade unions. When disputes occurred, Fowlers dealt directly with their men and avoided negotiating with the trade-union representatives:

> Q 25,752: Do you refuse to meet the men's representatives if they have them? – I do not think I should refuse, but if so I should certainly have them officially met by the Secretary of this union [i.e. the Secretary of the Leeds Engineering Employers' Federation]. But we have this feeling: we would rather give a little more to our own men than disturb the relations which have been so satisfactory for so many years.

On his admission, the level of engineers' wages was lower than in most other towns, but when challenged he put this down not to the strength of the Employers' Association and the contrasting weakness of the trade unions, but to the peculiar social-economic characteristics prevailing amongst the Leeds working class:

> We believe it [low wages] is caused by cheap houses, the desire which has grown up among working men to own their own houses, and the provident habits there; but probably more largely by the very great employment of women and children which exists in Leeds. I am told by working men representatives whom I talk to on this matter that a working man with a family is in a very much better position in Leeds in the matter of money at the week-end when the family earnings are added together than he is in Manchester or Wakefield or in surrounding towns, the trade which helps the family being very largely the ready made clothing trade.[14]

Competition from overseas rivals was putting severe pressure on the Leeds engineering trade. Fowlers was associated with the manufacture of agricultural machinery and competed with German, French and Belgian firms. Additionally, this part of their trade was seasonal in nature, and both these factors – seasonal demand and foreign competition – caused particular problems for the organization of the labour market. In his history of the engineering union, Jeffreys has outlined the developments which occurred: 'The twenty five years between 1890 and 1915 – particularly the fourteen years prior to the war – witnessed a minor revolution in the workshop, contrasting sharply with the relative absence of technical change between 1850 and 1890.'[15]

Another example of conditions in Leeds can be seen in the case of Edwin Kitson Clark, who entered the family business and described changes in the company between the late 1880s and the 1930s. In the mid-1880s, 'management was ... not by science but by personality ... In the shop of my first small command (the Bolt Shop) I followed an old gentleman who had worked his own system for forty years.' Over the next few years:

> a leading draughtsman ... came down into the works; it was considered an infraction of the boilermakers' craft but the change though in advance of recognised practice, was inevitable, and Kitson's Templet Shop was then shown with pride to visiting engineers: Under a specially light glass roof all plates and sheet patterns were marked out to an exact limit that I have never seen excelled ...[16]

Scientific management was being substituted for traditional shop-floor skill and improvization. New grades of planners and supervisors emerged to transfer design from the office to the shop floor via the job card. For the first time the skilled man could be ordered to 'Do as you are told; we do not pay you to think.'[17]

In July 1897 the changes and developments that had been slowly fermenting exploded in the form of a national lock-out of engineering workers. The thirty-four engineering companies which comprised the Leeds Federation of Engineering Employers (including the large concerns like Kitsons and Fowlers), issued lock-out notices to 1,900 ASE members, and 1,700 non-union men. Nationally, the issue was over the ASE demand for an eight-hour day and a general advance in ASE militancy, but the Leeds ASE did not make the eight-hour claim until after the lock-out was announced and put into effect. During the lock-out other issues emerged, including uncertainties about the question of picketing, and the willingness of employers to use 'free labour' against union labour. Whilst the ASE was becoming more militant, the engineering employers had developed a highly effective national organization. An Employers' Federation of Engineering Associations had been formed in June 1896, and had responded to the demand for an eight-hour day in the London district with a general lock-out. Late in January 1898 the union withdrew the demand, and the Employers' Terms of Settlement were imposed.[18]

The engineering dispute had demonstrated that even the strongest workers' union – the engineers – were weak by comparison with a well-organized employers' federation. Many learned from this the lesson that what could not be gained by industrial action might be won in the field of politics.

The clothing industry

The Leeds clothing industry was divided into two distinct but inter-dependent sectors: the English factory and the Jewish workshop. According to one estimate, there were 101 Jewish workshops employing 1,435 male and 447 female workers in 1891,[19] while another source puts the numbers at 64 workshops and 2,128 persons in 1894.[20] Conditions in Leeds were generally regarded as better than in other clothing areas; the worst features of the sweating system were not prevalent, and pay, conditions and hours compared well. The greater regularity of employ-ment among factory workers owed a good deal to the existence of the Jewish workshops, which bore the brunt of downturns in trade. The first recorded strike by Jewish industrial workers took place spontaneously in Leeds in May 1885 and was successful in gaining the reduction of the thirteen to fourteen-hour day by an hour. By 1887 approximately 750 workers were organised sufficiently to pursue a general strike in the Jewish trade the following year, which was, however, unsuccessful and which marked the collapse of the embryonic union.[21] The next attempt at organization occurred in the summer of 1889, when the socialists, with Isabella Ford, became involved in a strike of English tailoresses at the Arthur and Co. factory.

The traditional tailoring trade was catered for by the Amalgamated Society of Tailors (AST), which had been established in 1866 and which, twenty years later, had in Leeds a membership of 270, most of whom were skilled bespoke tailors, although a smaller number were skilled male cutters in the ready-made clothing factories.

The general picture is unquestionably one of an extremely weak trade-union presence in what had become, by the early 1890s, the major industry of the borough. This was true most of all among the tailoresses; despite the fact that between 13,000 and 15,000 women worked in tailoring or dressmaking their union never seems to have had more than about 200 members. Despite some small advances, wages remained low and virtually stationary throughout the whole period up to 1913–14. The industry was sharply divided between men and women, between skilled and unskilled, and between Jewish and gentile worker (see Table 7).

Table 7   Trade-unionism in the Leeds clothing industry, 1892–1904

Union	Year	Membership
Leeds Tailoresses' Union	1892	98
(formed 1889)	1893	212
	1895	40
	1897	62
	1898	31
Leeds Wholesale Clothing	1892	143
Operatives (formed 1889;	1893	271
amalgamated with other local		
clothing unions 1894)		
Amalgamated Union of Clothiers	1894	506
Operatives	1896	827
	1897	1042
	1898	990
Leeds Jewish Tailors', Machinists'	1893	272
and Pressers' Union	1895	492
(formed 1893)	1897	269
	1900	1150
	1902	1130
	1904	700

Sources: Report of Chief Labour Correspondent to the Board of Trade (1906), PP CXIII; Comparative Statistics, All Trades Unions, PP (1889), XCII.

There was also a good deal of resentment about the role of Jewish labour in the expanding wholesale and ready-made clothing sector, particularly amongst the traditional bespoke tailors of the AST. The existence of the Jewish workshops and, even more so, the estimated 3,000 or so women who worked in their homes gave the wholesale trade a vast advantage over the bespoke tailors. Before the Royal Commission on Labour of 1892 William Marston, president of the LTC and an AST member, was asked:

Is there such a thing as systematised immigration for the purposes of reducing wages?

– Very largely in Leeds, in many instances by the wholesale clothing manufacturers … I know the system is in existence in Leeds in the wholesale clothing trade by which vast numbers of men are brought over. Money is advanced by the manufacturer in the first instance to

workmen in his employ ... They send this money abroad to some of
their relatives. They are brought over and taken on as learners and the
money is repaid ... I think it is undue rivalry. Many of our best artisans have had to emigrate.[22]

The boot and shoe industry was classified as part of the dress and
clothing trade, but their trade union was better organized. The National
Union of Boot and Shoe Operatives (NUBSO) was formed as a break-
away from the old Cordwainers' Society, a consequence of the emergence
of the machine-made trade and the diminution of hand-made practices.
The NUBSO was built up in Leeds by John Judge and the appropriately
named John Buckle to be one of the strongest trade unions in the borough. As with engineering, the boot and shoe industry was facing stiff
international competition, particularly from America. The preferred
response of manufacturers was to introduce a new range of labour-saving
machinery, but it appears that, for a period, the union in Leeds was
strong enough to resist this innovation. Some manufacturers turned to
trading, importing boots for workmen from the United States. But the
main effect was a build-up of tension leading to conflict between
NUBSO and the employers' association.

The result was a general lock-out in all the federated areas, including
Leeds, from March 1895. Five weeks later the terms of settlement were
agreed which, *inter alia*, stipulated that there was to be no bargaining on
the 'introduction of machinery, or the output therefrom ...'[23] Following
the lock-out, union membership nationally declined dramatically from
43,000 in 1891 to 24,000 in 1906. In Leeds a new spirit of moderation
prevailed; the finishers in the factories were being replaced by machines
and the local Conciliation Board reported a unanimity of desire to press
forward with the implementation of the new machinery, although it was
recognized that the skill of the operative would no longer be necessary.

The parallel with engineering is striking, in that here, too, a whole area
of craft skill, status and prestige had been eroded or destroyed over the
decade 1895–1905.

Textiles

The textile industry declined both in relative importance and in absolute
numbers employed over the period 1870–1914. It was generally agreed
that trade-unionism in the industry was as badly organized as in ready-
made clothing, and that, in Leeds, the largest occupied section in the
trade, the power-loom weavers, were the worst organized section of all.
Jonathan Peate, a woollen manufacturer representing the Leeds Chamber
of Commerce before the Royal Commission on Labour, acknowledged
that there had been something approaching a 30 per cent increase in
output in Leeds without extra pay, and admitted that he knew 'so much

of what I consider very unjustifiable action on the part of the masters which could not be curbed or curtailed except by combination'.[24] However, unionism was slow to develop. Out of an estimated 150,000 textile workers in Yorkshire in the 1890s, only 17,000 were members of a trade union; in Leeds, out of the 22,000 people employed in textiles, probably no more than 2,000 were organised in trade unions. It was in weaving that the greatest intensification of work, accompanied by a reduction of piece-rates, took place. The introduction of the semi-automatic Northrop loom enabled savings on the unit costs of labour by making possible a two-loom system – one weaver could operate two looms. This was resisted by the better organized areas, including Huddersfield, but in Leeds the system was gradually introduced, without effective opposition, from the early 1890s.

Trade-unionism amongst the women workers was negligible. Across the whole of the Yorkshire textile industry at the end of the 1890s the total female membership was 1,291 at a time when, in Leeds alone, over 12,000 women were employed in the industry.[25] It was generally agreed that the women were employed to cheapen the price of men's labour. Both Isabella Ford and Gertrude Tuckwell agreed on this effect, and argued that the only remedy was trade-unionism.[26] A very effective barrier to the development of women's trade-unionism was the prevailing social attitude towards women's roles in the home. The *Yorkshire Factory Times* advised men not to marry mill girls, since home life suffered:

> The best wives for working men are those drawn from the ranks of domestic service … as Cobbett said if a woman is not afraid to be seen by her sweetheart up to her elbows in soap suds she will do. Upon her devolves the responsibility of financing the uncertain incomes of the family.[27]

It was from Maguire, and more consistently from Isabella Ford, that the pressure for women's trade-unionism came. Ford attacked the attitude of the men whose apparent chivalry disguised their real intention, which was not the admission of women into men's trade unions on equal terms, but rather was expressed in the idea 'Let us so restrict women's labour by kindly legislation that eventually women will be driven from the field altogether'. These attitudes were not confined to a few manual trade-unionists but pervaded the male mind in general.

Severe competition amongst employers in the Yorkshire textile districts, together with fragmented and weak trade-unionism, resulted in a great diversity in pay and conditions throughout the region. W. Yates, a worsted coat manufacturer, in evidence before the Royal Commission on Labour, claimed that £1 per week was the average earned by weavers throughout the Leeds district in the early 1890s. But the *Yorkshire Factory Times* and the union officials claimed that the weekly average, after taking fines into account, which were common for spoilt work, short-time working, seasonal fluctuations, and other stoppages, was nearer 13s. to 14s. (65–70p) per week. In April 1894 moves were made to set up a federation of all textile unions with the objective of standardizing pay and conditions for the large variety of textile grades throughout the Yorkshire district. The federation was in existence by the summer of 1894 but seems to have made little progress. It turned from the policy of industrial organization and advocated that conditions might best be improved by parliamentary regulation and legislation.[28]

From this survey of the main industries in Leeds, it is evident that the city's working class was deeply divided by trade, occupation, sex and racial differences. Competition within social class was as much a feature of working-class life as was the class unity for which socialists hoped. The function of political action came to be seen as removing working-class economic hardship and insecurity, and thereby creating the possibility of a class unity which could not often exist in the harsh economic realities of day-to-day life. Although the Leeds economy, because of its high level of diversification, may have protected the town from the worst effects of trade recession, and while it was the case that Leeds did not have a large and desperately impoverished casual labour force, it may be argued that such a group existed but was largely ignored because it was composed of women, and children working as half-timers. However, the issue of male and female economic roles and relationships did not become a major one in British socialist debate during this period.[29] It was only after decisive confrontations in traditional craft sectors, already traced in this chapter, that the Trades Council began to move and the basis was laid for an electorally successful independent labour party. Throughout the 1890s, craft trade unions found themselves coming off second best, beaten by effective employers' federations which pushed through technical change. At the same time, a series of legal decisions, culminating in the Taff Vale case, went against the unions.[30] Other sections of workers found themselves without effective workplace organization to prevent a deterioration of their conditions. By the late 1890s both groups were prepared to turn to Parliament and to politics in order to achieve what they were too weak to secure through industrial organization.

The ILP and the labour movement, 1895–1914

In Leeds, as in West Yorkshire in general, the Liberal Party dominated both parliamentary and local elections in the 1880s and 1890s. In the four general elections (1886, 1892, 1895 and 1900) Liberals won the vast majority of the 23 West Yorkshire constituencies, though their domination was beginning to show signs of being eroded after 1895. In the 1892 general election they took 20 parliamentary seats, while the Conservatives took 3; in 1895, and again in 1900, they took 14 compared to the 9 won by Conservatives. The general election of 1895 was the first one in which the ILP mounted a significant challenge to the Conservative and the Liberal Parties. Six candidates were fielded in West Yorkshire (Bradford West, Colne Valley, Dewsbury, Halifax, Huddersfield, and Leeds South) with Ben Tillett in Bradford performing best, taking 23 per cent of the poll, and Shaw in Leeds performing worst with 6 per cent. Although there was nothing here to frighten the Liberals, Laybourn and Reynolds have pointed out that some of the most significant Liberal losses to the Conservatives came in areas where the Labour challenge was strongest.[31] Nevertheless, in the short term the impact of the 1895 general election was a setback for the ILP. All 35 candidates fielded nationally were defeated, Keir Hardie lost his seat in West Ham, and branch membership declined. However, Laybourn and Reynolds have argued that, ultimately, the party came out of the experience to the good, more unified, realistic and tolerant than before. ILP branches might have been tempted to respond to the disappointment, they suggest, either by seeking an alliance with the Liberals, or by going the other way by seeking socialist unity with SDF branches. In the event, they continued to seek trade-union support for independent labour representation, while continuing a broadly based non-dogmatic form of ethical socialism, nurtured in the socialist Sunday Schools and the Labour Churches.[32]

Performances in parliamentary and local elections improved progressively. Having taken about 5 per cent of the poll nationally at the 1895 general election, and a little less in 1900, Labour candidates won 17 per cent of the votes in the 1906 general election, which 'marked the breakthrough of Labour into national politics'.[33] In all, 29 MPs, running under LRC auspices, were returned. In West Yorkshire 9 candidates were fielded, 3 of whom were successful (Jowett in Bradford West, Parker in Halifax, and O'Grady in East Leeds).

The Liberal Party also did well in the 1906 general election, increasing its parliamentary representation from 14 to 19. But the long-term signs indicating danger for the Liberals were very much present in the aggressive attack mounted by Labour in local elections. In Bradford the 6 Labour councillors had increased to 11 by 1906; in Huddersfield the 1 Labour councillor returned in 1900 was joined by a further eight in 1906; and in Leeds the first independent Labour councillor was returned in 1903 to be joined by 7 more by 1906. What Laybourn and Reynolds observed as the case for West Yorkshire in general was very much true for Leeds also: 'Labour was pressing Liberalism on all political fronts between 1906 and 1914 and there are few signs of Liberalism arresting the development of the ILP/Labour Party'.[34] We need now to turn to how this change came about in Leeds.

Leaders and ideas

The energies of the ILP in Leeds in its first years lay in the Labour clubs which existed in the Bramley, Armley, North East, East Hunslet, West and Holbeck wards. The West Ward Club, for example, had 264 members and the North East Ward had 100. Membership was on an individual basis and finance was pitifully weak. The central organization of the party was strengthened by the affiliation of all the ward clubs and in March 1893 T. B. Duncan was elected its first president. Duncan, born in Scotland in 1856, moved to Leeds and was a pioneer organizer of the Leeds Shop Assistants' Union. He was active in the Labour Church, the ILP and the LRC, and was noted for his moderation and tact: he claimed that he had 'never read a line of Marx or heard Hyndman speak'. Tom Maguire became the president of the Leeds ILP in August 1893 at the half-yearly meeting, and soon afterwards a new Leeds ILP Central Club was opened, in October 1894, by Keir Hardie.[35] The trade-unionists who had entered the movement in the years when Maguire was active remained as influential members of the party, but a new tone and a new membership was undoubtedly pervading the politics of the party. The vocabulary of the 'new testament' or ethical socialists began to be heard in the clubs. At the opening of the West Ward Labour Club, the Revd Westrope, a Methodist minister and new convert to the cause of socialism, felt that:

> [he] was convinced that the labour movement was a thoroughly and intensely religious one. He had the pages of history open before him and he had a conviction ... that God's work in history from the first day when Moses organised the first strike or at any rate struck the first blow for freedom ... down to the days of Ben Tillett ... [lay in the cause of the labour movement].[36]

Late in 1893 two new organizations were introduced into the local labour movement: the Labour Church, opened in September 1893, and the Leeds Social Reform Union (LSRU), the latter aiming to bring together 'men of all creeds who were united in wanting to make conditions in Leeds better ... They were pledged to no party. They had no sectarian or party animus or bias. They simply met on the grounds of common humanity ...'[37] The LSRU seems to have been an attempt to coax the LTC to work with people with advanced ideas on social reform, without the political commitment to the ILP which the leading Liberals on the Council were strongly resisting. The Leeds Fabian Society, formed by Marles and Mattison in 1891–92,[38] was in part the result of a vacuum left by the collapse of the Socialist League and provided a forum in which nationally significant issues could be debated. It did not have a widespread impact on the movement locally but, over the years, it did serve to provide a venue for the discussion of cultural issues, about the relation between art and democracy; George Bernard Shaw, for example, visited the city in 1909 at the invitation of the Fabian Society and the Arts Club and gave a talk, in which he argued that the theatre was increasingly the source of modern ideas and an essential part of a modern democratic community.

An attempt was made by the ILP in 1894 to provide a kind of impressionistic survey of the range of social problems prominent in Leeds following the manner of the 'discovery of poverty' accounts which had occurred in the East End of London during the 1880s. The document is an interesting one, revealing as it does a marked change in political tone and emphasis. The survey, entitled *Hypnotic Leeds*, provided a glimpse of the conscience of the Leeds ILP in the early 1890s demonstrating its concern for a range of social issues from crime and gambling, alcoholism and prostitution, through to housing, education, art and literature. *Hypnotic Leeds* set out to appeal to all classes for the good of society, presenting a politicized moral and social crusade against the selfishness of all classes, a call for all people to wake up to a sense of social and public duty. I suggested in Chapter 4 that the ILP drew its support from a broader social base than the industrial working class, and that its pragmatic proposals for social reform were surrounded by a wider appeal based on a broad conception of socialism which went beyond economic interest and motivation. By the middle of the 1890s a new white-collar group was emerging to provide leadership of the party. John Badlay was an insurance agent who in 1913 became a director of the Royal Liver Insurance Society. He was very active in ILP politics from the mid-1890s, and was president of the party on two occasions up to 1914, becoming leader of the Labour group on the town council. Joseph Burgess (Leeds ILP organizer in the late 1880s) was a journalist, and Leonard Verity and D. B. Foster (see below) were both small businessmen. Verity was an optician, with his own shops in Leeds and Harrogate. He was active in Leeds ILP politics from 1904, and was adopted as the West Leeds prospective parliamentary candidate in 1912. Another activist was Isabella Ford, who became a member of the ILP National Administrative Council. She was a member of a prominent Quaker family from middle-class Adel, with a tradition of activity in issues of social reform. She dedicated herself to efforts to organize the tailoresses of Leeds, and was an executive committee member of the National Association of Women's Suffrage Societies. Further examples of white-collar activists in the ILP include Joseph Clayton (an Oxford graduate), Ethel Annakin, Edward Pease, Mary Gawthorpe and Alfred Orage, all of whom were schoolteachers.

Orage was one of the most remarkable intellectuals associated with the city. Born in 1873 at Dacre Bank in North Yorkshire, he qualified as a teacher and took up a post with the Leeds School Board at Chapel

Allerton in 1893. He heard Tom Mann speak in Sheffield and joined the new ILP in Leeds, contributing to the *Labour Leader*, the national newspaper of the ILP, between 1895 and 1897. In this period he was an enthusiast for the ideas of Walt Whitman, William Morris and Edward Carpenter, but his philosophical quest led him to form a Leeds Theosophical Society and a Plato study group, where he met the architect A. J. Penty. With Penty and S. G. Hobson he was later to develop the ideas of guild socialism (see Chapter 6), and from 1900, under the influence of Nietzsche's *Thus Spake Zarathustra*, he formed a passionate commitment to find a 'new morality for new men'.[39] Tom Steele has written the history of Orage's cultural and political influence nationally, beginning with his formation, with Holbrook Jackson, of the Leeds Arts Club in 1903, 'one of the most interesting sites of radical thought and experimental art outside London'.[40] The ILP Central Club and the socialist Clarion Club which Orage had joined provided a venue for working-class militants to come into contact with socialist intellectuals like Edward Carpenter and Isabella Ford. Similarly, the Leeds Arts Club provided a meeting place where those who were politically active could gather new ideas, and where those who were from the business community mixed with 'artists and writers with dangerous ideas [which] offered more than a frisson of excitement', challenging received Victorian values on art, religion, morality and sex. Echoing Carpenter, the club was dedicated to 'life as experiment', and following Morris, 'nothing that was neither useful nor beautiful was allowed through the doors'.[41] In 1906 Orage left Leeds for London, where he took over the magazine *New Age* and transformed it into one of the most influential cultural and political weeklies in England.

Despite the richness of this discourse, these perspectives did not immediately become part of normal branch life, although the long term impact, while hard to measure, was profound. The social base of the club was the 'professional proletariat' – teachers, architects, journalists, typographers, illustrators, photographers, professional painters, musicians and clergymen. Along with the experimentation with culture, art and ideas, the club was also engaged in the definition of citizenship:

> For them citizenship was bound up with creating the City Beautiful, a two way process in which beautiful cities were the materialisation of beautiful ideas, and ideals, which in turn produced beautiful people. The city was the building block for the decentralised state, autonomous and democratic, it would be a noble, dignified and above all healthy environment for its citizens of the future.[42]

This definition of modern citizenship was grounded in the objectives of the local socialists in the ILP to capture local government. The concept of municipal socialism was a positive one in the thinking of British socialists in the early twentieth century: town and city councils were seen as more democratic than Parliament and provided the focus for a new era of democracy. In municipal socialism socialists saw a direct means of satisfying the vision of new community:

> for we see shining in the distance
> the lights of our new Jerusalem
> the city whose wealth consists not in
> the fortunes of its mills, but in the
> health and happiness of the men and
> women who inhabit it.[43]

D. B. Foster epitomized the political values of the Leeds Labour Party, spanning its history from 1893 when he joined the ILP to the period when, in the years up to 1914, he was he was the full-time secretary of the local Labour Party. The development of Foster's political ideas and career provides a good illustration of that blend of ethical Christian socialist motivation, tempered by a pragmatic consideration for electoral advantage which guided the LLRC up to the First World War. Foster was born in 1855 in Holme, Spalding Moor, in the East Riding of Yorkshire, and was apprenticed in a draper's business in Pudsey. His parents were active Wesleyans and he became a local preacher at the age of seventeen. In 1885 he moved to Leeds where he had purchased a business and where, in the big city environment, he experienced a degree of intellectual stimulation that was new to him and which generated an interest in social and political issues. He began to question dominant Wesleyan religious teaching and, when he took charge of the Sweet Street Mission, encountered directly the economic and social problems of industrial South Leeds. Late in 1890 Foster responded to these experiences by joining the Holbeck Liberal Party and he was subsequently involved in the formation of the Holbeck Social Reform Union. His involvement with the Liberals was short-lived: 'During this period I felt an increasing dissatisfaction with the Liberal Party as I discovered its incapacity for voicing the needs of the working classes'.[44]

In 1893 Foster broke with the Liberal Party and, disappointed by the small impact of the Holbeck Social Reform Union, joined the newly formed Holbeck ILP. With characteristic vigour, he committed himself fully to the party. In 1895 and 1896 he ran as a candidate in the municipal elections, achieving a disappointingly low vote. Undaunted, he continued his involvement and, with Alfred Orage, who was its main editor, took part in the production of *Forward*, a monthly news-sheet aimed at the Leeds electorate. *Forward* was eventually handed over to the official party organization under the editorship of Joseph Burgess. Participation in the activities of the Labour Church was a logical progression for Foster, his main concern being to create a religion of socialism, fusing the spiritual feelings which had guided him with an awareness of the economic realities of industrial Leeds. Applying his socialist convictions to his own lifestyle, he decided to give up his business and dedicate himself full time to the socialist cause. He continued to fight local elections for the ILP through the late 1890s without any success, and took to free-lance propaganda work. The main objective of his propaganda was to develop a Christian socialist awareness 'in order to help the free thinking socialist to a realisation of the intrinsic value of the teachings of Jesus, and on the other hand to help the bewildered Christians out of the labyrinth of orthodox creeds'.[45] At this point, in the closing years of the century, Foster was as much interested in the practice of a socialist lifestyle as in the popularizing of socialist ideas. Following the emergence of Tolstoyan ideas, he visited the Brotherhood Community in Purleigh,[46] and late in 1897 became involved with the formation of the Brotherhood Workshop in Victoria Road, Holbeck. The failure of this co-operative workshop resulted in the return of Foster to political work. By 1900 he was well known in the socialist movement locally and became, for a short period in 1902, secretary of the new LLRC. However, he soon left this post as his interests returned to the religious-spiritual as opposed to the organizational aspects of the movement. Between 1903 and 1905 he devoted his energies to, and became president of, the Labour Church but abandoned this as well, this time in favour of Unitarian preaching, when he judged that the Labour Churches were not 'God conscious' enough. He gave up Unitarianism in turn, when his congregation became hostile to his political views, and resumed his political work, fighting four municipal elections between 1907 and 1910, before finally winning West Hunslet in 1911. In 1912 he became full-time secretary of the Leeds Labour Party, an important and influential post which he held until 1916. By this time he had interpreted his enthusiasm for public service in the Labour cause as a means of fulfilling his Christian responsibilities: 'socialism and the Christ are one', he declared, and his church became the Town Hall, which he regarded as 'the House of God'.[47] Mary Gawthorpe, a young teacher who became involved with the ILP in the late 1890s and later with women's suffrage, was one of a number who entered the movement driven by the same motivations as Foster.[48]

Foster was deeply concerned about what might now be called 'lifestyle politics' but he also saw the importance of efficient and large-scale political organization and did not regard the two areas of activity as contradictory. He was one of the main exponents locally of the labour alliance in socialist politics, and of the need to gain as much electoral representation as possible with trade-union support. He justified the alliance on the basis of a theory of class-consciousness which united all the elements in a common quest for socialism, but in which some groups and some individuals had reached a higher stage than others. In his view the trade unions had a natural tendency towards socialism rather than towards liberalism, despite the fact that, historically, they had achieved their aims through the Liberal Party. Trade-unionism aimed at the replacement of individual bargaining with collective bargaining, and embodied the principle of collective rather than individual action. Yet the trade unions, he argued, only represented a stage of development in the labour movement called craft-consciousness. There is a link between craft-consciousness and progress towards class-consciousness:

> After removing competition between the individual workers by the formation of trade unions, the workers proceed to eliminate competition between the different trades by the introduction of federations, so leading up to the effective organisation of the workers in one class conscious community ...

Beyond class-consciousness lay race- or social-consciousness, the final stage in human evolution. Foster then envisaged a rather mechanical four-stage evolution from individual- to social-consciousness, and within this schema he regarded consciousness as a matter of individual conversion:

> Here we have the real danger to the Labour Party, and the great opportunity of those who have attained to a fuller social consciousness. The danger is that a man who has become craft (or trade) conscious only may refuse to pay the cost of further growth, which will make him a constant irritation and hindrance to those who are working towards trade federation, or the larger class consciousness. Similarly ... the class conscious man may, and often does, refuse to pay the cost of becoming conscious of his unity with those who have hitherto formed the capitalist class ...

The consequence of the first position is to remain locked within the narrow limitations of trade-union issues and Liberal politics; the consequence of the second is to join socialist politics and bitterly denounce capitalism without seeking solutions. The most difficult transition to make is 'the socialisation of the personality when class hatred is overcome and complete human solidarity realised'. It is through experience in or association with the labour movement that such conversion may be realized. The task of the Labour Party is to foster social- rather than class-consciousness within the movement, and at the same time 'develop social consciousness in the British electorate to such an extent that they will vote for the application of our principle to legislation'. In this view, class-consciousness is defined as a stage which must be transcended by the Labour Party, by the realization of socialist policies, through parliamentary legislation, in the interests of the whole nation.[49]

Socialism was, then, both an economic and a moral-intellectual development, depending for its realization not only on the material needs of the working class but also on the conversion of the professional middle class. In this way, the role of class in politics was redefined. For a while in the 1880s the Leeds socialists had come under the influence of the ideas of Morris and the Socialist League, for whom socialism meant class conflict made conscious. The fear that the working class would lose any revolutionary capability the more they were granted reforms was the recurrent concern in Morris's thought. Parliamentary and electoral activity was to be avoided, since the working class should be mobilized not for elections but as a counter-cultural force. This type of political view did not become deeply rooted in Leeds. The socialists of the period 1885–90 themselves turned to the politics of reformism because of the lack of response from the working-class community, and indeed it was the material conditions of this community that determined that social welfare policy would dominate.

Of all the first-generation socialists who joined Maguire in the Socialist League in 1885, only one, Alfred Mattison, remained active in local labour politics through the period of the formation of the Labour Party, and beyond that to the first Labour government in 1924. Although never a leader of opinion, Mattison was a lifelong observer of labour politics and personalities. He was born in 1868 in Hunslet, his father a skilled engine-fitter, and, although little is known about his parents, they enjoyed a fairly secure existence, living not in a back-to-back but a through-terrace house in Carey Street, Hunslet. Mattison joined the Socialist League in the spring of 1885 and entered into what was probably his most active political phase between the period 1885–95, when the movement was small but about to establish itself amongst important sections of the working class. He was, for a short period in 1890, the secretary of the Leeds branch of the GGLU and joined with Maguire and Mahon in the attempt to bring the trade unions under the influence of socialist electoral politics. He attended the first General Conference of the ILP as a delegate from East Hunslet, and was a member of the Fabian Society. In 1893 he became one of the first secretaries of the Labour Church. Until the late 1890s he worked as an engineer at the Hunslet Engine Company and then left to take up an administrative position at the Tramway offices.

Mattison met Edward Carpenter through the Socialist League, and Carpenter became his friend, guide and philosopher, particularly during the 1890s. In the 1890s Mattison visited Carpenter frequently at his home at Millthorpe near Sheffield, and some of the essence of what it meant to be part of the socialist movement, promoting the cause with a crusader's enthusiasm, is captured in Mattison's notebooks and correspondence. In April 1894, for example, he went with Carpenter to Baslow, a mining village near Millthorpe, and recorded:

We made half a dozen visits to the miners' houses and in every case were kindly received. We would talk on many matters, their work, its nature, their alas! in many cases – lack of work. A little interest displayed in their lives went such a long way, as E. C. bid them not to lose heart in the struggle. Would speak of things not being as they might be, and incidentally tell of the movement that was going on in the towns amongst the organised workmen to better their social position. We took a quantity of old labour and socialist papers, leaflets, and pamphlets for them to read. Once or twice we succeeded in getting quite a little meeting in one or other of the houses; and then we brightened up matters by singing a socialist song – E. C. and I leading off ...[50]

In Carpenter's view the cause of socialism was advanced through the fellowship of comrades and the evolution of a new consciousness. At the same time this did not exclude the need to build a successful electoral party – a need which Carpenter not only acknowledged but worked for. Mattison, in common with many others in the movement as a whole, increasingly placed his efforts in the building of the party rather than in pursuing Carpenter's quest – a quest which perhaps Mattison never fully understood. For him, the cause was realized in the defeat of the 'old gang' of trade-unionists who supported the Liberal Party, and crowned in the late 1920s when, for the first time, a majority of socialists controlled the Leeds city Council: 'In this hour of triumph let us remember those pioneers who scattered the seed of socialism so many, many years ago.'

At the same time as organizing the vote the LLRC developed a new preoccupation with demonstrating that it was capable of undertaking the responsibilities of public government. Class conflict and industrial action were not interpreted as forces which generated revolutionary consciousness in the Marxist sense. On May Day 1912 James O'Grady, the Labour MP for East Leeds, told his audience: 'We are the only class who are not a class for we are the nation'.[51] The function of the Labour Party was not to release class aggression but to transcend it. The judgement of the community expressed through the vote provided the ultimate justification for policy and action and the purpose of socialism was to unite the efforts of classes in the true interests of the nation.

Membership

It was recognized that the ILP in Leeds had mixed fortunes and slow growth after the foundation boom of 1891–3. When the national conference was held in there in 1899 it was observed that: 'Leeds was not reputed an auspicious town in which to hold the annual conference of the ILP. The ILP has not prospered there ...'[52]

Table 8 illustrates the fluctuation in party membership, which fell from 1,000 in 1894 to a low of between 25 and 72 around the turn of the century. Stimulated by the formation of the LLRC and successes in local elections between 1903 and 1906, the membership grew again and stabilized at around an average of 160 between 1906 and 1914. In the period between 1905 and 1914 Leeds ILP branch membership always remained a numerically small part of the total LLRC membership.

Table 8   Leeds ILP branch membership by selected years, 1893–1914

Year	Membership	Year	Membership
1893	400	1901	25
1894	1,000	1905–6	290
1897	257	1909–10	155
1898*	228	1911–12	170
1898†	72	1912–13	147
1899	150	1913–14	147
1900	25		

*Spring; †December.

Source: ILP *News*; ILP Annual Conference Reports; Leeds LRC Yearbooks, 1906–1914.

A large part of the problem was put down to the reluctance of the trade unions to come over to independent labour politics *en masse*: 'Until Trade Unionism, at any rate, is prepared to move, much progress on Parliamentary lines is impossible. Till it does, we shall have to be content to wait ...'[53] Leeds trade-unionism made this move in the closing years of the century and, despite the numerical weakness of the ILP, its members were strategically well placed. Although by the mid-1890s the influence of Maguire and Mahon on socialism in Leeds had ceased, it had been important to the new generation of trade-unionists who had come into the movement in the early 1890s, and who now played a decisive role in guiding the trade unions into support for ILP politics. Walter Wood, for example, became involved during the 1890 gas strike and in the subsequent moves to form the local ILP. He acknowledged that he owed his socialism to Maguire and, as the first president of the Leeds GGLU and as a paid official of the union for the rest of his working life, he was a prominent promoter of the ILP on the Trades Council. J. E. Smith, secretary of the GGLU, followed the same path, becoming, like Wood, a socialist through his experience of the 1890 strike. From an Irish background, he was a member of the Irish Nationalist League and was instrumental in securing Irish support for James O'Grady in East Leeds in the 1906 general election. Arthur Shaw, a member of the ASE, joined the ILP in 1894 and has the distinction of being the first ILP candidate to run in a general election in Leeds, contesting the South Leeds constituency in 1895. Shaw was also the first member of the ILP to become president of the Trades Council (defeating the Lib–Lab representative William Marston in 1895). Smith and Wood successfully moved the resolution by which the Trades Council agreed, in 1897, to open a political fund to support labour candidates in elections, a decision which was encouraged by the defeat of the ASE in the lock-out of that year.[54] Shaw was chairman of the ASE lock-out committee and was clear in delivering the political message of the event: '… they must reorganize their society and make it a powerful political force'.[55]

The ground was well prepared by these three ILP trade-unionists for the formal embrace of independent labour politics. In February 1900 Shaw was a delegate to the LRC foundation conference in London. In June of that year the LTC, under the presidency of Wood, voted to affiliate to the new organization.

The labour alliance: the ILP and the Leeds Labour Representation Committee

Although it was the LTC which voted to affiliate to the LLRC, it was the socialists of the central ILP club in Briggate who took the initiative in determining the form which the local organization would take. Despite its small membership, individual members of the party were sometimes colourful and always influential in Labour politics. J. D. Macrae was party secretary in 1902 and LLRC secretary from 1907 to 1910. Before him, D. B. Foster (the second secretary of the ILP after its formation) was LLRC secretary for a short while, taking over again on a full-time basis in 1912. John Badlay, ILP secretary in 1901, became one of the first Labour and ILP councillors in Leeds and leader of the Labour group on council. These men, because of their political acumen, energy, and commitment, had an influence in the LLRC far beyond that justified by the extent of party membership.

The LLRC was emerging more clearly as a distinct political force by the winter of 1902. However, D. B. Foster commented in 1902 that, although the bulk of labour movement activists were in favour of a policy of independence, 'we have a fairly strong element of Liberal Labour people in the Trades Council who wish to work under the Liberal wing'.[56] Consequently, the first five years of the LLRC were marked by a manœuvring for position. The main protagonists were Owen Connellan and John Buckle, representing the liberal tradition of the LTC on the one hand, and the 'independents' on the other, principally Wood, Macrae and Foster, all ILP members seeking to gain both control of the LLRC and the political backing of the LTC.

The key conflict emerged over the proposed candidature of Owen Connellan for the East Leeds constituency. Connellan's candidacy was actively advocated by the East Leeds Liberal Association and by Connellan's own trade union, the Leeds Typographical Association whose Secretary, R. M. Lancaster, put the case directly to the National Labour Representation Committee (NLRC). What worried Connellan's supporters in Leeds, however, was that, if he were to go to the poll, he would be unlikely to get the support of the LLRC because of his 'position as a Liberal councillor and being allied with the official party'.[57] At the same time the LLRC, through its new secretary J. D. Macrae, was also in contact with James Ramsay MacDonald and was concerned above all that, whatever candidate was selected, he should not be under the influence of the Liberal Party. A struggle developed over the issue of which organization (and hence which political affiliation) should control the direction of the political activity of the labour movement in Leeds. At its conference on 10 April 1904 the LLRC selected James O'Grady as its parliamentary candidate for East Leeds, awarding him 121 votes as opposed to Connellan's 48.

Shortly after this decision the lobbying began, when Connellan's supporters questioned the authority of the LLRC not to endorse him, following his selection by the LTC. To resolve the dispute, MacDonald nominated a deputation from the NLRC to meet representatives from the LTC, the LLRC, as well as O'Grady and Connellan. J. D. Macrae saw all this manœuvring as more than a conflict of personalities: 'The local LRC as an organisation is at stake and the time has come for striking out straight, the kid glove methods having failed. The most noticeable feature is that the same element fought against the formation of the LRC, both locally and nationally.' [58]

Those who, like Connellan, wished to develop the political activity of the labour movement with the goodwill of the Liberal Party found themselves the victims of a rapidly developing independent and socialist organizational upsurge centred on the LLRC, which was far less inclined to compromise with liberalism than was the NLRC. Connellan and Marston, the old guard, were desperately trying to retain their leadership of the traditional Lib–Lab axis which still predominated on the Trades Council. Despite the protests of Connellan, the parliamentary Labour candidate selected by the LLRC for East Leeds was confirmed by MacDonald, and the political authority of the LLRC was established. This decision effectively promoted a further dispute between Leeds and London, since the LLRC, straining at the leash, was not content with the one contest in East Leeds and wished, additionally, to run candidates in the West and South Leeds constituencies. This was very much against the intentions of MacDonald, who argued forcefully that the LLRC should concentrate on one contest and warned them against over-extending themselves. Above all, it appears, MacDonald was anxious that anti-Liberal action of the kind envisaged by Leeds would spoil the efforts that he was making in secret to reach an electoral pact with Herbert Gladstone as Liberal Chief Whip, specifying an agreed number of constituencies where the LRC might have a free run. What happened in Leeds was clearly of importance nationally, since Herbert Gladstone was also the MP for West Leeds and he did not wish his own constituency to be the subject of LLRC interest. This, however, was exactly what the LLRC intended, blissfully ignorant as they were of any national pact being negotiated by MacDonald.

The LLRC went ahead, and at a special conference on 26 November 1905 selected Albert Fox to stand for South Leeds.[59] Of much more concern to MacDonald was the news that the LLRC, bolstered by municipal victories in wards within the Leeds West constituency, was considering running W. T. Newlove against Gladstone in West Leeds. MacDonald's reply was quick and threatening:

We have a very strong national responsibility on our shoulders. When we recommended Mr O'Grady's society to allow him to go to Leeds it was on the understanding that only one candidate was to be run and we shall probably have to communicate with his executive on the present situation. Judging however from what I have heard my executive will even go to the length of publishing a condemnatory resolution in the newspapers if you insist locally on a third candidate.[60]

While expressing some surprise at this, the LLRC did finally back down in the face of national pressure and accepted what was, in fact, a compromise: Fox and O'Grady were to be run, while Herbert Gladstone, at least on this occasion, was to be left alone.

The LLRC: organization and membership, 1903–1914

By late 1905 the LLRC had won some important struggles for status and recognition in the Leeds labour movement, particularly in diminishing the importance of the older Lib–Lab influences within the Trades Council. It had established itself on the principle of the labour alliance – the unity of socialist and labour organizations – as the major legitimate party of organized labour in the city. Organizations entitled to affiliate to the LLRC were identified as follows:

(a)   All local trade-union branches.
(b)   Co-operative societies, specified as the Leeds Industrial Co-

operative Society; the Beeston Co-operative Society; the Leeds
Trade Union Co-operative Society; the Farnley Co-operative
Society; the Unique Clothing Society; the Leeds Builders Ltd.
(c)   Political groups, specified as the Leeds Fabian Society; all Leeds
branches of the SDF; all local ILP branches; all branches of the
Irish Nationalists; and the Leeds Labour Church.

By the spring of 1903 over 10,500 people were affiliated to the LLRC
through their respective organizations, forty-seven of which were trade-
union branches, including the LTC. Amongst the co-operatives, only
the Trade Union Co-operative Society had affiliated. From the third
category – the political groups – came the Armley Social Democratic
Federation, the Fabian Society, four ILP branches (Central, North, South
and West), and the Labour Church. In terms of members affiliated, the
trade unions supplied a weighty preponderance of LLRC membership
from the earliest years. By 1906 the organization had grown by about
3,000, and a breakdown of membership according to the three groups
defined as the organizational constituency for the party provides a useful
insight into the developing membership structure.

**Table 9   Leeds Labour Representation Committee membership,
1906**

	No. of branches	Total membership	% of total
Trade unions	72	12,565	92.0
Co-operative societies	1	40	0.3
Political groups			
LRC ward branches	10	652	
ILP	6	294	
Fabian Society	1	20	7.7
Women's Labour League	1	60	
South Leeds Socialist Union	1	60	

Source: Leeds LRC Annual Report, 1906.

Table 9 illustrates the very small organized socialist influence in the new
alliance in proportion to overall affiliation to the party. The trade unions
accounted for over 90 per cent of LLRC affiliated membership in the
delegate meetings; those affiliated directly through political organizations amounted to only 8 per cent of total membership. Thus, ILP
affiliated membership formed only 2 per cent of the LLRC total, and

the SDF, based in Armley, formed at most 0.5 per cent. The influence of
the Fabian Society was, as might be expected, numerically very slight,
and it appears that this membership was generally inactive, certainly far
less significant than the ILP and SDF.

**Table 10   Leeds Labour Representation Committee membership,
1912–1913**

	No. of branches	Total membership	% of total
Trade unions	59	11,468	88.0
Co-operative societies	1	30	0.2
Political groups			
ILP	3	147	
LRC ward branches	8	860	
Local socialist organizations	5	390	12.0
Women's Guilds and Labour Leagues	5	105	

Source: Leeds LRC Annual Reports.

In common with the labour movement nationally, the local party suffered the consequences of the 1909 Osborne judgement which made it
illegal for a trade union to provide for parliamentary representation by
means of a compulsory levy. Internally, problems were caused by disputes
between unions and the expulsion from the party of Wood, Buckle and
Wilson, the former for supporting Catholic educational demands, Buckle
and Wilson for supporting the visit of the King to the city in 1908 – both
of which went against party policy. For all these reasons, membership
fell and, between 1909 and 1913, major efforts had to be put into
sustaining organization and finance (see Table 10).

From the winter of 1913 prospects seemed good, owing to the oper-
ation of the 1913 Trade Union Act, which removed the restriction of the
Osborne judgement. D. B. Foster as party secretary, pointed to the need
to recruit and organize more effectively: 'There are yet some 50 trade
union branches unaffiliated with the Party, there are several wards in
which no Party organisation exists ... and the very large number of
unattached sympathizers in the city must be brought into active membership with us.'[61] The LLRC was able to support the new independent
labour newspaper the *Leeds Weekly Citizen*, which had appeared as a
weekly since September 1911, financed by shares issued to labour movement organizations and activists in the city. Additionally, the SDF,

reformed as the British Socialist Party, became affiliated to the LLRC in 1913, and its most active members – Harold Clay and Ruston Bert Killip – were immediately elected officials of the party.

The general committee of the LLRC was, in fact, the general meeting of delegates from affiliated organizations. Day-to-day business was carried out by an executive committee elected by and from this meeting. Ward LRCs were encouraged to handle the groundwork necessary for municipal election work. Ten wards had local LRC organizations by early 1906.[62] The function of the ward committee was to canvas and organize the labour vote, and it also had the power to recommend candidates for municipal elections to the LRC centrally. The post of party secretary was one of the most influential, a position that was made permanent and salaried in 1910 and was filled (following financial defaults by J. D. Macrae and his successor H. A. Newell) by D. B. Foster in September 1912. In April 1914 the LLRC formally agreed to change its name to the Leeds Labour Party.[63]

The impact of the LLRC on parliamentary elections

In 1885 Leeds was divided into five parliamentary constituencies in such a way that the working-class vote dominated the South and West constituencies (both south of the River Aire), and the East constituency. When, as a result of the Gladstone–MacDonald agreement, the Liberals stood down from the East Leeds contest in 1906, the seat then became the only one secured by Labour in the period up to 1914. North and Central, previously Conservative, were taken by the Liberals in 1902 and 1906 respectively and remained Liberal in 1910. By the general elections of 1906 and 1910 Leeds, as it was represented in Parliament, was more firmly a Liberal city than it had ever been.

A review of electoral issues between 1885 and 1895 has already been presented in Chapter 2. Arthur Shaw, the first ILP candidate to go to the polls in a general election in Leeds, had fought unsuccessfully in South Leeds on an anti-Liberal platform. His appeal relied on socialist solutions to trade-union problems. In 1895 such an appeal had been premature and Shaw secured less than 7 per cent of the poll. He had come into the field very late and the labour vote was not organized behind him. North and Central constituencies were dominated by commercial and professional groups. North Leeds was gaining about 700 voters per annum through the growth of Roundhay Road and the development of housing in Burley and Headingley, where a large proportion of new voters were said to belong to 'the class of superior artisans and the lower middle classes'.[64] The race was on to win the votes of these people. Central Leeds was a peculiar division, where majorities were small. It was, essentially, a commercial constituency comprising not only the large warehouses and principal business offices, but also some of the poorest living areas of Leeds, inhabited by one of the poorest sections of the population, the newly arrived Eastern European Jews. The number eligible to vote was small, but the Jewish vote was an important one, since majorities tended to be narrow.

W. P. Byles was the next ILP candidate to run, at the 1900 general election in East Leeds. Byles had worked on the *Bradford Observer* and took over the management of the paper from his father in 1891. Supporters of the ILP who were also active in the Irish National League had made the initial approach to him, and he based his campaign on the removal of legal obstacles to trade-unionism, introduction of old-age pensions, an attack on the foreign policy of the Salisbury administration and an assertion of the justice of Home Rule for Ireland. The 1900 election was conducted in an atmosphere heightened by emotional issues released by the Boer war. Despite this, the result of Byles' campaign was not without encouragement for future independent Labour prospects. He came last in a three-cornered contest but he secured a respectable 20 per cent of the poll, in spite of divisions surrounding his selection. Byles was, in fact, not a member of the ILP and Laybourn has identified him as a progressive liberal (indeed, perhaps the only significant advocate of new or progressive liberalism in West Yorkshire) who wished to forge an alliance with the ILP.[65]

At the 1906 general election, and the 1908 South Leeds by-election, James O'Grady, the LLRC candidate in East Leeds, and Albert Fox, ASLEF general secretary and LLRC candidate in South Leeds, both put forward an advanced programme of social reform, although O'Grady's position was more clearly a socialist one, whereas Fox denied that he was a socialist and stood as an 'advanced labour' candidate. Both candidates advocated free trade, free education, free school meals, old-age pensions, payment of MP's and women's suffrage, and gave priority to unemployment as a problem to be tackled. O'Grady – inevitably in East Leeds, the heartland of the Irish community – was in favour of Irish Home Rule. However, the social reform interest of the Labour candidates was, in large measure, an end in itself, whereas, in the socialist theory of the late 1880s and early 1890s, social reform had been regarded as an integral part of a transitional process leading to a more radical kind of socialist society.

For the Labour Party candidates, in so far as social reform had an objective beyond its own inherent humanity and necessity, it was to serve the needs of nation and empire, rather than the process of working-class self-emancipation. O'Grady, for example, spoke out against bad housing, poverty, and unemployment because:

No empire worth dying for can be held together by a home country peopled ... by a few extravagantly rich and a vast number miserably poor ... I am therefore of the opinion that in the interests of the Empire as well as of our own county the business of the coming parliament is with social reform.[66]

In the 1906 general election the Liberal Party gained its most impressive victory ever. In West Yorkshire as a whole the Conservatives failed to win even one of the twenty-two seats. But an analysis of the share of the poll reveals a more complex pattern. What happened was that middle-class Conservative voters switched to the Liberals, while a significant number of working-class Conservative and Liberal voters switched to Labour. The combined Conservative and Liberal Unionist votes had fallen by 20 per cent with 12 per cent of this going to Labour (O'Grady and Fox) and 8 per cent to the Liberals. In Leeds these trends were expressed as shown in Table 11.

Table 11   Share of the poll in Leeds at the general elections of 1900 and 1906 (%)

	1900	1906
Liberal	43.9	51.4
Liberal Unionist	13.2	
Conservative	40.2	33.8
Labour	2.5	14.5

Labour in municipal politics

While the decline of liberalism was not evident in the distribution of parliamentary seats in Leeds by 1914, its problems were very clear at the grass roots, in local politics. The ILP benefited greatly in terms of electoral success from its membership of the LLRC and the support of the affiliated trade unions which came, as we have seen, in the early years of the new century. The ILP was involved in thirteen separate municipal contests between 1893 and 1900 and was unsuccessful in all of them, taking a percentage share in the poll, in the wards fought, in the range of 3 per cent and 19 per cent. By 1907, on the other hand, Leeds had five councillors elected under LLRC auspices, who were also members of the ILP: George Layton, a locomotive driver and ASLEF member, brother-in-law of the late Maguire, represented East Ward; John Badlay, GGLU official and insurance agent, East Hunslet; T. C. Wilson, a laundry worker and member of the Shop Assistants' Union, West Hunslet;

J. D. Macrae, LLRC Secretary and ASCJ member, Armley and Wortley; and A. Shaw, member of the ASE, New Wortley (Shaw had fought South Leeds for the ILP in 1895). D. B. Foster, who had first fought Holbeck for the ILP in 1895, finally won West Hunslet in 1911, the year before he became the LLRC Secretary. The improvement in electoral performance was remarkable once the ILP had trade-union backing through the LLRC and it is no surprise that in Leeds the party remained a staunch supporter of the labour alliance.

A branch of the Marxist SDF (which had been originally formed in Leeds in 1884 but seceded to become a branch of the Socialist League) was operating again by the winter of 1896–7, based in Armley. In 1908 the SDF changed its name to the Social Democratic Party, and, as part of a drive to socialist unity, the name was changed again to the British Socialist Party (BSP) in 1911. The annual meeting of the Leeds ILP in April 1912 considered its views on socialist unity and decided that, although the BSP and ILP had similar objectives, the difference was that the ILP had found it necessary to combine with the trade-union movement in order to make any progress. In the vote on socialist unity in 1912, every Leeds branch of the ILP remained loyal and turned down the option of merging with the BSP.[67]

From 1903 onwards the LRC and the ILP actually had a group of councillors with a responsibility for policy in local government, an issue on which the party needed to develop a firmer view. In 1904 the LLRC issued a manifesto which was to determine the policy priorities of the first Labour councillors on the city council. A leading plank of this manifesto was a call for the extension of municipal services, including municipal banking services, and coal and milk supplies. In addition to these enterprises, the council was to act as a model employer, setting high standards of employment which private business would be forced to emulate.[68] Local politics was not regarded as less important than national politics, but was seen as providing a crucial arena for the emergence of socialist activity. The potential to attack the values of *laissez-faire* capitalism, to develop a positive concept of citizenship for the new democracy and, at the same time, to engender the emergence of a socialist economy, was seen to be great at local level.

The LLRC began to direct its addresses to the small business sector as well as to the working-class community. In 1912 it was making a special appeal to the clerk, the shop assistant, the manager, the commercial traveller and the small tradesman to come into the Labour Party to protect themselves from commercial monopolies:

Hitherto the small tradesman has fought shy of the Labour Party, believing that their policy was one of increasing rates. Let us examine his position. He is being gradually but surely eaten up by the Trust or Combine …

Our policy of increasing the worker's wages means increasing his spending power; and that means more takings for the small trader ...[69]

The emphasis on municipal enterprise was itself based on a vision of the democratic city and was as capable of attracting the aesthetic interests of the white-collar and professional worker as it was the economic interests of the poor or the trade-unionist. This was one area of policy which exposed a division between the Labour Party, on the one hand, and the Liberals and Conservatives, on the other. A second major area of polarisation lay in responses to the industrial militancy which built up in Leeds from the summer of 1911. During the national strike of railway workers in that year, the Liberal government sent soldiers to Leeds at the request of the railway companies, an act immediately condemned by the Labour Party, whose candidates made full use of the issue. D. B. Foster campaigned in West Hunslet (a ward with a heavy concentration of railway employees) against the use of the military in strikes, and held the ward for Labour. The position taken by the Liberal government also alienated trade-unionists from within its own party. In the winter of 1911–12 the Watch Committee decided to form a Special Police Reserve force which, in the view of the LLRC, was intended primarily as a strike-breaking force. Labour Councillor F. Gath claimed that 'the trade unions were seriously contemplating organizing a counter force to fight the Council police if need be'.[70] This heightened class-awareness was dramatically expressed in April 1914 when a crowd of 4,000 assembled in Victoria Square at the call of the LTC in support of Tom Mann, who was threatened with imprisonment for his 'Don't Shoot' speech, in which he had called upon soldiers not to use force against workers on strike. R. Escritt, for the LTC and the LLRC, called on workers not to join the Army until they knew that they would not be called upon to act against trade-unionists. In December 1913 a strike of municipal employees broke out and threw into clear relief the issues dividing the Labour Party from Liberals and Conservatives. The strike was precipitated by a wage demand, but was immediately elevated into a symbolic political struggle by the reaction of the dominant Conservative group and its leader Charles H. Wilson.[71] The strike was defeated, but the LLRC drove home the accumulating examples of clashing Liberal and trade-union interests. The progressive Liberal newspaper, the *Yorkshire Observer*, angrily denounced the failure of the Liberal councillors to distinguish themselves sufficiently from the Conservatives, whose policy was not to find a solution to the strike, but to defeat the strikers. The Liberals could have taken a useful and genuinely middle-ground position, acting as a mediating force and promoting a solution through collective bargaining and conciliation. Two weeks into the strike, the GGLU was hinting about its desire for a meeting to reach a compromise, which the Liberals could have facilitated. Instead, they joined with Alderman Wilson and the Conservatives in a crusade against socialism. Although the Liberals formally repudiated any idea of an alliance with the Conservatives, in a statement issued in February 1914 and signed by all prominent local party members, the LLRC continued to criticize the Liberal Party for working in association with the Tories, despite their assurances to the contrary.

Table 12   Wards won by Liberal, Conservative and Labour candidates in local elections, 1890–1913

	Councillors			Aldermen			Total		
Date	Con.	Lib.	Lab.	Con.	Lib.	Lab.	Con.	Lib.	Lab.
1890	18	30			16		18	46	
1891	24	24			16		24	40	
1892	21	27			16		21	43	
1893	24	24			16		24	40	
1894	28	20			16		28	36	
1895	30	18		8	8		38	26	
1896	25	23		9	7		34	30	
1897	25	23		9	7		34	30	
1898	22	26		16			38	26	
1899	22	26		16			38	26	
1900	21	27		16			37	27	
1901	20	28		16			36	28	
1902	18	30		16			34	30	
1903	18	29	1	16			34	26	1
1904	13	32	3	7	8	1	20	40	4
1905	12	29	7	7	8	1	19	37	8
1906	14	26	8	7	8	1	21	34	9
1907	21	18	9	7	8	1	28	26	10
1908	29	15	3	7	8	1	36	23	4
1909	27	15	5	7	8	1	34	23	6
1910	24	18	5	7	8	1	31	26	6
1911	19	20	9	7	8	1	26	28	10
1912	26	15	10	8	8	1	34	33	11
1913	25	12	14	9	6	2	34	18	16

Sources: Leeds Official Yearbook; Morrison's Leeds 'Blue Book' and City Record; *Leeds Mercury.*

Table 12 illustrates the electoral effect of the emergence of Labour as an independent force in local politics. By 1913 Labour had more elected councillors than the Liberals and were prevented from being the main opposition party to the Conservatives only because of a disproportionately high allocation of aldermanic seats to the Liberals. The Labour challenge was strongest in the traditional Liberal strongholds. Between 1900 and 1913 Labour candidates fought 106 contests, of which 30 were successful. West Hunslet was overwhelmingly Liberal from 1881 until 1904, when it was captured by Labour for the first time. The same was true for East Hunslet, which was Liberal throughout the period to 1903 (with the exception of 1894) after which it was almost as firmly Labour. Holbeck, East and North East wards also displayed a strong movement to Labour. In other wards the Liberals were holding on in the face of stiff Labour opposition, or losing to the Conservatives because the Labour candidate had split their vote (in Armley and Wortley, and the West, for example). The Liberal Party was losing ground seriously in its traditional south-of-the-river stronghold and in the East and North East wards north of the river. The portents were clear in their indication of the insecurity on which the Liberal parliamentary majorities were built. The traditional geographical and social areas of Liberal support were weakening, while no commensurate impact was being made in the mixed wards or in the dominantly Conservative wards of South, North Central, Brunswick, Mill Hill and Headingley. The work of the socialists, initiated in 1887 with the Handbill for a Socialist Labour Party (and the forebodings of Mathers, the Liberal Party agent, voiced in 1895), had come, at least in part, to fruition.

Notes

1. R. C. K. Ensor, *England 1870–1914* (Oxford, 1936), p. 266.
2. Cited in Tom Steele, *Alfred Orage and the Leeds Arts Club 1893–1923* (Aldershot, 1990), p. 219.
3. K. Laybourn and J. Reynolds, *Liberalism and the Rise of Labour 1890–1918* (London, 1984), pp. 106–7.
4. K. Laybourn, *The Rise of Labour: The British Labour Party 1890–1979* (London, 1988), p. 25.
5. *Ibid.*, p. 16.
6. *Ibid.*, p. 24.
7. *Ibid.*, pp. 22–3.
8. *Ibid.*, p. 24.
9. See W. G. Rimmer, 'Occupations in Leeds 1841–1951', *Thoresby Society Miscellany* 14, 2 (1967).
10. *YFT,* 4 August 1893 and 10 August 1894.
11. *YFT,* 3 February 1899.
12. *Royal Commission on Trade Unions*, Eleventh Report, PP (1864–9) XXXI, pp. 286–7; *YFT,* 17 December 1897, and 31 August 1900.
13. *YFT,* 16 October 1891.

14. *Royal Commission on Labour (RCL)*, (1893–4), XXXII, pp. 357 and 796.

15. J. B. Jeffreys, *The Story of The Engineers* (London, 1946), p. 132.

16. E. Kitson Clark, *Kitsons of Leeds* (London, 1938) pp. 151–4.

17. Jeffreys, *Story of the Engineers*, p. 132.

18. *Ibid.*, p. 148. Research has focused on authority divisions within enterprises, centred around the concept of the labour process. Examples include H. Braverman, *Labour and Monopoly Capital* (London, 1974), and something of this approach is used by J. Foster, *Class Struggle and the Industrial Revolution* (London, 1977). I have used this approach in the analysis of the engineering industry in Leeds, but it might be fruitfully extended in the form of a more systematic survey of industrial relations in Leeds industries, building on the industrial histories started by Rimmer.

19. L. P. Gartner, *The Jewish Immigrants in England, 1870–1914* (London, 1960), p. 88.

20. J. Thomas, 'A History of The Leeds Clothing Industry', *Yorkshire Bulletin of Economic and Social Research*, Occasional Paper No. 1 (1955), p. 20.

21. Gartner, *Jewish Immigrants in England*, p. 118.

22. *RCL*, Group C, Vol. I, PP (1892), XXXV, p. 394.

23. A. Fox, *A History of the National Union of Boot and Shoe Operatives, 1874–1957* (Oxford, 1958), p. 232.

24. *RCL*, Group C, Vol. I, PP (1892), XXXV, p. 917, and pp. 316–22.

25. Comparative Statistical Tables, Female Trade-Unionists, PP (1899), XCII, pp. 691–3.

26. *Ibid.*, See, for example, I. Ford, 'Industrial Conditions Affecting Women of the Working Classes', *YFT*, 17 March 1893; and G. Tuckwell, 'Competition Among Manual Workers', *YFT*, 13 November 1898.

27. *YFT*, 5 December 1890.

28. *Ibid.*, 13 and 27 April 1894.

29. The observation that Leeds did not have an impoverished underclass was made in the Royal Commission on The Housing of The Working Classes, PP (1885), XXXl, p. 325. On sexual roles, see the discussion of Edward Carpenter's ideas on socialist and sexual issues in S. Rowbotham and J. Weekes, *Socialism and The New Life* (London, 1977); and the discussion of prostitution by A. Marles, in *Hypnotic Leeds* (Leeds, 1894).

30. See J. Saville, 'Unions and Free Labour: The Background to the Taff Vale Decision', in A. Briggs and J. Saville (eds), *Essays in Labour History* (London, 1960).

31. Laybourn and Reynolds, *Liberalism*, p. 70.

32. *Ibid.*, p. 95.

33. *Ibid.*, p. 132.

34. *Ibid.*, p. 143.

35. At the first annual conference of the Leeds ILP Maguire was nominated for the presidency against Duncan, but was defeated. Connellan was vice-president of the ILP in its first year. *YFT*, 3 March 1893 and 26 October 1894.

36. *YFT*, 20 January 1893.

37. *YFT*, 12 January 1894.

38. The programme of the Fabian Society for the period January–March 1893 suggests that evolutionary ideas were entering the movement and

apparently peacefully co-existing with the Marxism of Mahon. Under the Fabian programme Mahon lectured on 'Marx's explanation of the Cause of Poverty', and J. Dyche on 'Marx's Theory of Value'; in the same series Marles lectured on 'Illustrative Readings from Miss Potter's Cooperation'. Of all the lectures recorded as part of the Leeds Fabian Society series, only Maguire's 'The Evolution of a Great Thing' is preserved and this does reflect a strong reforming orientation.

39. Entry on Orage in J. Saville and J. Bellamy (eds), *Dictionary of Labour Biography*, 6 (Basingstoke, 1982) p. 199.

40. Tom Steele, *Alfred Orage and the Leeds Arts Club 1893–1923* (Aldershot, 1990), p. 1.

41. *Ibid.*, p. 258.

42. *Ibid.*, p. 260.

43. H. Russell Smart, *Municipal Socialism* (Manchester, *c.*1895), cited in M. Cahill, 'Socialism and the City', in T. Jowitt and R. Taylor (eds), *Bradford 1890–1914: The Cradle of the Independent Labour Party* (Bradford Centre Occasional Papers 2, 1980), p. 48.

44. D. B. Foster, *Life Story* (Leeds, 1921), p. 26.

45. *Ibid.* p. 39.

46. See W. H. G. Armytage, *Heavens Below* (London, 1961).

47. Foster, *Life Story*, pp. 59 and 63.

48. M. Gawthorpe, *Up Hill to Holloway* (Penobscot/Traversity Press, 1962), pp. 173–4.

49. Quotations in this paragraph are from D. B. Foster, *The Logic of The Alliance: Or, the Labour Party Analyzed and Justified* (Leeds, 1911). For a discussion of the role of class in politics in this period see J. F. Whelan, 'The Working Class in British Socialist Thought', M.Phil thesis (University of Leeds, 1974).

50. A. Mattison, *Notebook* 1 (1894), p. 6.

51. *YFT*, 11 May 1912.

52. *ILP News*, April 1899

53. *ILP News*, October 1898.

54. Trades Council subscriptions were increased and one quarter of the increase was to be available to support political representatives. There was no condition laid down that representatives should be independent of the Liberal or Conservative Parties; they merely needed the approval of the Executive Committee of the Trades Council. *YFT*, 3 December 1897.

55. *YFT*, 21 January 1898.

56. LRCP 6/252; Foster to MacDonald, 4 December 1902.

57. LRCP, 13/262; R. M. Lancaster (Secretary, Leeds Typographical Association) to MacDonald, 13 February 1904.

58. LRCP 14/215; Macrae to MacDonald, 7 May 1904.

59. 104 societies were represented at the conference by 166 delegates. LRCP 28/213; Macrae to MacDonald, 26 November 1905.

60. LRCP 28/216; MacDonald to Macrae, 6 December 1905.

61. LLRC Minutes, 5 May 1914.

62. These were Armley, Bramley, New Wortley, Holbeck, West Hunslet, East Hunslet, East Leeds, North West, West and Headingley.

63. LLRC, Group and Executive Committee Minutes, 16 April 1914.

64.   *Yorkshire Post*, 10 July 1895.
65.   K. Laybourn, *The Rise of Labour: The British Labour Party 1890–1979* (London, 1988), p. 28.
66.   See *YFT*, January 1906 issues.
67.   Leeds ILP Federal Council, Annual Meeting, reported in *Leeds Weekly Citizen* (*LWC*), 6 April 1912.
68.   LRC, 'A Review, Some Reasons, and a Policy' (1906).
69.   *Ibid.*
70.   *LWC*, 20 January 1912.
71.   For a full account of this, see J. E. Williams, 'The Leeds Corporation Strike in 1913', in A. Briggs and J. Saville (eds), *Essays in Labour History 1886–1923*, Vol. II (London, 1971).

Chapter 6

Jerusalem? The Politics of the Labour Alliance

The vision of co-operative production and ownership of the means of life came to me as the dawning of the morning. Here I saw the way to the Kingdom of God on earth for which I had prayed and worked for so long ... my outlook on life was fundamentally changed ... I saw that the new Jerusalem was a possibility.

D. B. Foster, on joining the Leeds ILP, 1893.[1]

It is impossible to build up a scheme for the society of the future for no man can really think himself out of his own days: his palace of days to come can only be constructed from the aspirations forced upon him by his present surroundings, and from his dreams of the life of the past ...

William Morris, 1893.[2]

The Liberal vs. Labour debate revisited

The very success of the electoral alliance between the ILP and the trade unions, embodied in the Labour Party, presented a dilemma for those ILP members who were motivated by more Utopian visions of a new community and a new democracy, who felt their socialist convictions as a force stronger than political pragmatism and the need for welfare reform. For them, the liberty tree needed nourishment to provide not only economic and political, but cultural fruits also. This concluding chapter surveys the diversity of ideas which informed labour and progressive thinking in Leeds in this period and, in doing so, considers the variety of what Howell, following Barrington Moore, has called 'suppressed alternatives'.[3] To begin this survey we must deal with a debate that has occupied historians for a number of years. Its essence is that the Labour Party itself formed no kind of alternative, and that by 1914 the Liberal Party actually encompassed the politics of Labour in a progressive alliance.

This debate is an important one because it sheds light not only on the origins of the Labour Party, but also on its nature, and this in turn affects expectations of what it might be capable of in the present and future. Historians have provided competing explanations to account for the decline of liberalism and the rise of labour and the debate has been evaluated by Keith Laybourn.[4] For some, the explanation lies in the impact that the First World War had on the Liberal Party, causing internal conflict which led to its weakness and collapse. If this explanation is followed, then the Labour Party succeeded because it filled a vacuum created by the failure of liberalism which, in turn, was the outcome of poor judgement and leadership by Liberal politicians, rather than the effect of trends and changes which occurred before 1914.[5] In Wales and the North East, for example, it has been shown that traditional liberalism, based on the values of international peace, free trade, limited government, and religious Nonconformity, remained electorally strong in the period up to 1914.[6] Clarke has argued that in Lancashire a political tradition of so-called new liberalism, based on a commitment to social and welfare reforms, was the cause of Liberal electoral dominance of that region before 1914. Duncan Tanner also argues that, by 1914, the Labour Party was not in as strong a position to challenge the Liberal Party as some historians, keen to prove that class politics were secured in this period, have made out.[7]

Tanner's thesis is that the Liberals responded to the formation of the Labour Party as an alliance between the socialists and the trade unions in 1900 by developing a tacit electoral alliance with the new organization. This alliance enabled Labour to emerge as a junior partner in a progressive alliance between the Labour and Liberal Parties. The agreement which made this possible – the Gladstone-MacDonald pact of 1903 – was forged between Herbert Gladstone, Liberal Chief Whip and MP for the West Leeds parliamentary constituency, and James Ramsay MacDonald, leader of the NLRC. The pact was an unofficial agreement to allow Labour candidates free runs in up to fifty-two constituencies, without Liberal opposition; in return, MacDonald was to encourage Labour organizations not to put up candidates in opposition to Liberals in other seats. At the same time, although there were tensions between different sections, liberalism had developed a belief in social justice, welfare and community which did not subvert traditional liberal loyalties to individualism. This ideological development (known as new liberalism), combined with an electoral accommodation with Labour, provided the basis for a new politics – in Tanner's phrase a 'Progressive Alliance'. Yorkshire was a key centre for testing the viability of such an alliance. As Tanner says: 'Yorkshire was of paramount importance to both Progressive parties. It was a Liberal stronghold, which had to be retained. It was also the birthplace of the ILP, and the single most important area of its activity and development.'[8] Although admitting a great deal of local variation, Tanner's argument is that by 1914 a progressive alliance in Yorkshire held firm. He suggests that traditional Gladstonian liberalism and the new liberalism emerged in a radical/centrist alliance which was electorally successful. On the other hand Labour failed to 'create a truly dynamic and positive "left-wing" appeal'; the party made most of its progress in Leeds and Bradford, he suggests, before 1906 when Liberals were extremely conservative. After 1906, as the practical socialism of the Labour Party began to converge with the new Liberal social reform outlook, Labour victories came as much from operating within the progressive alliance context as from the attractions of the Labour Left.[9]

While this account adds a great deal to our understanding of the complexity of the politics in this period, the experience of Leeds tends to confirm the opposing perspective presented by Laybourn who, building on what he refers to as the Pelling–McKibbin 'Labour School',[10] argues convincingly that, when one looks at what was going on in the localities, and particularly at patterns of local elections, the base of Liberal support amongst working-class communities was eroding. Most importantly, a new political culture and sentiment was emerging in working-class communities. In terms of providing vision and policy, it is not clear that new liberalism was so successful in other parts of the country as it appears to have been in Lancashire. It was not an important force in London[11] and Laybourn suggests that it was not a force in the West Riding of Yorkshire. This observation is broadly true for Leeds as well: there was a form of progressive liberalism which had a hold on those involved in the labour movement in the 1870s and 1880s, but it failed to develop as a significant political force. New liberalism did not feature significantly in Leeds politics before 1914 and Liberals tended to offer a narrow budget-balancing view of local government which moved them into an alliance with the Conservatives. Liberalism lost its sense of vision and its ability to inspire and motivate politically. In Bradford, Keighley, Huddersfield and in Leeds, 'Liberalism ... was aggressive, abrasive and unwilling to compromise with labour'.[12]

So far as Leeds is concerned, then, we must conclude this debate with the observation that well-established bases of support, on which the Liberal Party in the city had historically depended, had been breached locally by a confident labour movement which had fashioned its own alternative to a narrow local liberalism. In making this comment, it should be observed that liberalism in Leeds had not always been so narrow and defensive. The discourse conducted during the 1870s about the vital issue of power and balance in industrial communities, and about co-operative association as a meaningful form of economic democracy and autonomy which did not necessitate the expansion of state power, was an important tradition in progressive liberalism which had itself become a 'suppressed alternative' in the politics of the emergent Labour Party. And yet, there was a need for such a discourse. In his study of politics in Leicester,[13] Bill Lancaster has shown that the nature of the industries specific to the town affected working-class political culture. Mechanization of production – virtually guaranteed after the success of the manufacturers' boot and shoe operatives lock-out in 1895 – turned hand-workers into machine-operatives, while sharper international competition meant that by 1900 Leicester was beginning to experience long-term unemployment, particularly amongst adult male footwear-workers. From this context, a programme of municipal socialism, as offered by the ILP, provided an attractive political option in response to local poverty. As we have seen, this is exactly what happened in Leeds. But, argues Lancaster, older, political sentiments for autonomy persisted, so that: 'in 1900 the Leicester labour movement still had one foot in each century. It is true that locally the need for the palliatives of welfare reform were gaining expression, but many still clung to older solutions, especially land reform and agricultural colonies.'[14]

As the figurehead of the Leicester LRC, James Ramsay MacDonald was able, by 1905, to build support in local elections, capitalizing on the growing concern about unemployment. MacDonald's election to parliament in 1906 'sealed the consolidation of class-based Labour politics in Leicester'[15] and by this time the organizational decline of the Liberal Party was also evident. However, the tension between the needs for autonomy and independence on the one hand and the collective politics of parliamentary reform on the other was not wholly eradicated. The same ambiguity emerged in Leeds, and helps to explain the resistance of Lib–Labs like John Judge, Owen Connellan, and William Marston to the collectivism of the new Labour Party. Old notions of radical liberalism, going back to the days of James Hole and the co-operators, and to R. M. Carter and the co-operative communalists, had taken this need for economic democracy and autonomy very seriously. In the modern history of the labour movement the desire for measures for workers' control emerged at different times as the Labour Party pursued its parliamentary road to socialism.

Guild socialism and other critiques of the parliamentary road

To a degree, Tom Maguire, John Mahon and the Socialist League had attempted, in the period 1885–90, to construct a political programme which rooted socialism not in state policy, but in working-class and communal forms of self-activity. This attempt failed, but other groups were represented in Leeds and need to be considered. Anarchists, syndicalists and guild socialists were all concerned to develop political activity which did not depend on electoral machinery directed towards the control of state policy. In particular the anarchist tradition was vigorous at times in Leeds and the claim may also justly be made that the origins of guild socialist ideas lay in part in discussions held in Leeds around the turn of the century.

Anarchist ideas in Britain emerged around discussions in the papers *Anarchist* and *Freedom* in the mid-1880s, and they influenced the Socialist League, stressing anti-parliamentary activity, a hostility to the role of a central authority and a positive view of voluntary co-operative activity. During the 1890 gas strike in Leeds, the anarchists on the Socialist League began to consider 'revolutionary warfare', following the view of David Nicholl that 'individual assaults on the system will lead to riots, riots to revolts, revolts to insurrection, insurrection to revolution'.[16] In fact, Maguire and the political socialists channelled the new unionist energies released by the corporation strikes in 1890 into trade-union organization and socialist electoral politics. The trial and imprisonment of the Walsall anarchists in 1892, the increasing resort to propaganda by deed and the suspicion of *agents provocateurs*, all resulted in the late 1890s in very little open anarchist activity, because of a growing association with nihilistic violence. In Leeds Billy MacQueen and Matt Sollitt (who had been a member of the SDF and the Socialist League) did continue with open air propaganda, advocating the international general strike. Rudolf Rocker, a Jewish clothing worker, union organizer and anarchist, described Leeds in 1901 as an active centre of Jewish anarchism.[17]

By the late 1890s, however, anarchist hopes of revolution had diminished, and energies went instead into the development of co-operative communities. MacQueen edited a paper, the *Free Commune*, and the opening of a Tolstoyan inspired co-operative colony at Purleigh provided the inspiration for a co-operative in Leeds – the Brotherhood Workshop – which made bicycles and electrical components. The workshop was originally set up for men like Arthur Shaw, who had been blacklisted after the 1897 engineers' lock-out, but, as D. B. Foster recorded, they did not stay with it, 'so it was started by a few comrades gathered from various parts ... There is no recognition of "fair" or "equal" division of wages. Each ... takes from the treasury such as they need ...'[18] The Brotherhood Workshop did not survive for long as a co-operative enterprise and seems to have been taken over by Foster who had, in the summer of 1898, visited the Purleigh colony and immediately seen in it a means of realizing his ideal of Christian socialism. However, the short life of the Brotherhood Workshop in Leeds, combined with the scathing hostility of the ILP to 'Brotherhoodism', moved Foster back into electoral politics. This hostility was based on the belief that: 'The first step in civic progress ... is to rehabilitate the State ... only by civilising and socialising the State can man become truly civilized and social ...' Brotherhoodism, on the other hand, depended on anarchists and 'somewhat saintly Tolstoyans who are inclined to lie abed in the comfortable belief that if only all is well with their own soul and body that is enough ...' In another ILP article (giving the example of the Beeston

Brotherhood in Leeds, a development from the co-operative workshop which refused to recognize state authority) Foster concluded that: 'Such escapades in "Brotherhood" have absolutely no relation to Socialism or the Civic Communism of our ideal.'[19] At the end of the century MacQueen emigrated to America, and by 1913 Sollitt (at the age of 74) was found to be living in extreme poverty.

The anarchist tradition of opposition to officialism, the advocacy of direct action and the general strike emerged again in the form of syndicalism in the early years of the new century. The history of British syndicalism has been dealt with by Holton who, while pointing out that its impact on the labour movement was limited, nevertheless showed how syndicalist ideas contributed to an understanding of a number of processes not systematically confronted by the parliamentary socialist groups. In particular, syndicalists placed emphasis in their writings on the negative aspect of technological change displacing skill in the work process, the problem of trade-union bureaucracy, and the dangers of bureaucratic state capitalism. Guy Aldred's Industrial Union of Direct Actionists, committed to building new revolutionary industrial unions and to workers' control of industry, had some support, according to Holton, in Leeds and Liverpool, where a number of radical stonemasons promoted syndicalist ideas in the provincial building trades.[20] The Leeds municipal strike of 1913 was also referred to as inspired by syndicalism, but it was more the case that the militancy of the strike, which involved some minor cases of sabotage, was the result of the attempt of the GGLU leadership, heavily committed to electoral representation and institutionalized industrial relations, to re-assert their authority in the face of competition for membership, particularly with the rapidly growing Workers' Union. While the LLRC, the BSP and D. B. Foster all warned against the damage that the growth of direct action ideas and anti-parliamentary attitudes might have, overall the syndicalist impact was marginal. The LLRC had gone through a period of slow growth between 1907 and 1910, and by 1912 it had recovered well and was developing rapidly with the support of the vast majority of members of the organized labour movement. Militant trade-union action in Leeds in this period tended to be associated with the consolidation of Labour Party strength, rather than with extra-political activity.

Guild socialism, associated with A. J. Penty, A. Orage, S. G. Hobson and Holbrook Jackson, while not opposed to parliamentary activity, stressed more the importance of economic self-regulation, economic democracy, and the protection of craft skill and status. Orage met Arthur Penty, an architect from Knaresborough, in 1900, and found that they shared the same concerns. This group considered the formation of a William Morris society, an intention which actually took shape as the Leeds Arts Club, a discussion group whose function owed a great deal to the values of Morris (see Chapter 5). Its first syllabus declared: 'The separation of use from beauty or beauty from use proves in the long run disastrous for both.'[21]

In 1905 Orage moved to London and, with Jackson, took control of the weekly review *The New Age*, at that time edited by Joseph Clayton as an ILP journal. Clayton had been in Leeds in the 1890s. Through this journal, the ideas of Orage and Penty were developed to the distinct features of guild socialism, which was, in part, a resurrection and adaptation of the ideas of Morris and a criticism of political trends in the labour movement. Penty published his ideas on production in small-scale trade guilds in his book *The Restoration of the Guild System*, and the theme was taken up by Orage in an article in *Contemporary Review* in 1907. This was a perceptive critique of labour politics, in that Orage stressed the complete failure of the socialist movement to take seriously the ideas on craft skill raised by William Morris and John Ruskin. Those who, in the 1880s and 1890s, were motivated by the ideas of the Arts and Crafts movement joined with the socialist movement, which by 1906 was pursuing largely economic goals under the influence of the trade unions, rather than the aesthetic goals whose objectives were the qualities of craft production and control. Orage continued: 'it is necessary to protest against the exclusive association of socialism, which in its large sense is no less than the will to create a new order of society, with the partial and class prejudiced ideas of the working man ...'[22] As Orage saw it, socialism should not be identified with labour politics only, since its limitation to the special needs of the workman resulted in more collectivism; by contrast, the demands of the craftsman for good work had been largely ignored. He concluded with an attack on the collectivist vision of mass production, and a call for local markets, small workshops and restricted machinery. These ideals soon emerged in the form of guild socialism in the pages of *New Age* and in the book edited by Orage, but based on the work of S. G. Hobson, *National Guilds: An Inquiry into the Wage System and the Way Out* (1914). These ideas took political form with the setting up of the National Guilds League in 1915, but with the removal of Orage from Leeds in 1905 this current of thought ceased to have any practical significance in the politics of local socialists.[23]

The Social Democratic Federation and the British Socialist Party

There had been frequent calls to form a single socialist party, principally from the ILP and the SDF. William Morris had made an attempt in the early 1890s and Robert Blatchford, through the *Clarion*, ran a campaign to unite the two parties from the mid-1890s.[24] In Leeds the first branch of the SDF was formed in September 1884, but its influence on the socialist policies of the town did not last long. In the dispute which broke out around Christmas 1884 Leeds socialists followed William

Morris, John L. Mahon and others into the Socialist League (see Chapter 3). For a large part of the 1890s, then, the SDF did not have a foothold in Leeds.

In a major new study, Crick argues that the importance of the SDF in the history of the British labour movement has been misunderstood and underestimated.[25] Contrary to its received image as a dogmatic Marxist sect led by the authoritarian and egotistical H. M. Hyndman, Crick argues that it developed as a mature socialist organization which had adapted well to the British political environment and which played an important part in key moments of political development. This can certainly be said to be true of Leeds, though some might accuse it here of adapting too well to the British environment since the Leeds branch was keen on an alliance with labour, with or without socialism. Nationally, the SDF was a pioneer of the socialist revival of the 1880s and participated in the formation of the LRC in 1900 and in the drive for socialist unity from 1909. It was probably the main source through which Marxist ideas entered the British political tradition. Yet Crick argues that its strengths were in London and the cotton towns of Lancashire, not in West Yorkshire where it was, by comparison, a failure in terms of membership, not least because it was confronted by a strong ILP, busily forging an alliance with the trade unions on the basis of labour rather than socialist unity. The West Yorkshire ILP was at the head of the opposition to socialist unity after 1895.

The SDF was re-formed in Leeds in 1896–97, with its stronghold in Armley, and a Central Leeds branch was added by 1900. They tended to content themselves with weekly propaganda meetings and established a socialist institute around which a social life developed, but they seem to have kept themselves remote from trade unions. The appointment of Bert Killip as SDF organizer in 1907, according to Crick, revitalized the organization in the city. Three new branches were formed, a trading department marketing 'Red Flag' toffee was set up, and Killip went on the offensive against what he saw as the limited objectives of the labour movement in the city, believing that a red-blooded socialism should be proclaimed. To further this, and seeing himself very much as a Leeds version of Victor Grayson (Grayson was one of the first MPs to be selected on an overtly socialist ticket – in Colne Valley in 1907), he took on Owen Connellan in the council elections of 1909, taking great delight in taking the seat, though Killip's own vote was a tiny 168.[26] When Grayson called his Socialist Unity conference at Manchester in the autumn of 1911 and the SDF became the British Socialist Party, Leeds was represented by the Leeds BSP, the North and West Leeds branches of the SDF, the Burley ILP and the Leeds Clarion Scouts. However, there were no significant ILP defections and in April 1913 the BSP in Leeds decided to affiliate itself to the Labour Party, accepting labour unity as more viable than socialist unity. It is clear that the Armley SDF was strongly in favour of pursuing electoral work within a broader alliance of the kind embodied in the LLRC organization. When the SDF nationally withdrew from the LRC shortly after its formation, the Armley branch made an unsuccessful attempt to persuade the national executive to hold a referendum of the membership on rejoining the LRC. There was a period from 1906–11, following the departure of the SDF from the LRC, when a considerable degree of bitterness and public hostility between the two organizations broke out, particularly at election times. The SDF (or the SDP as it had become by 1908) developed a policy of putting up candidates at municipal elections particularly against LRC men who were running on a labour rather than a socialist ticket.

The position of the BSP left it open to recurrent charges that it was anti-trade union, charges which, however, it was well able to refute: 'The BSP is not anti-trade unionist. True, we are constantly pointing out the inadequacy of trade unionism in itself to realize the workers ideals.'[27] BSP members were fully involved in local industrial militancy in the years between 1911 and 1914. The party was prominent in the organization of the Workers' Union at local levels, and the union was recruiting manual workers who were becoming dissatisfied with a growing conciliatory attitude among the leadership of the GGLU. By 1913 the Workers' Union had recruited over 1,000 members in Leeds and the proposal that it should be allowed to affiliate with the LTC was moved by Harold Clay, a BSP member.[28]

There was a full municipal strike in 1913 and BSP members were again prominent.[29] All this, however, was a question of degree. In the end, the BSP in Leeds had far more in common with the LLRC than it did with the varieties of syndicalism that were developing.[30] Early in March 1913 the BSP discussed its attitude towards the Leeds Labour Party and the resolution to affiliate was moved by Clay. While it was accepted that the local Labour Party was as advanced as the BSP in terms of its municipal programme and candidates, the doubt arose in relation to the Labour Party nationally. Nevertheless, the affiliation was carried by a two-thirds majority and at the meeting of the LLRC Executive Committee on 10 April 1913 the West Leeds BSP formally applied for membership, 'stating that their affiliation was understood by their members to apply to the local Labour Party and not to bind them to support the national labour candidates'. This caveat gave rise to an animated discussion at the meeting of the Executive Committee, the majority of whose members, however, came out in favour of the BSP. At an LLRC general meeting on 17 April it was pointed out, after national advice had been taken, that it was unconstitutional to accept an affiliation which refused to recognize national Labour Party authority. Despite this advice a large majority of the 102 delegates present endorsed the original decision of the Leeds party executive to accept the affiliation.[31]

It was, undoubtedly, the West Leeds branch, based in Armley and Burley, that was the most vigorous centre of activity. It had a strong sense of the need to be rooted in the community and to set up worker controlled enterprises:

> There is nothing to prevent the bulk of our incomes being spent through societies which are or can be controlled by the workers themselves. In clothing there is the Co-operative Supply Association; in footwear we have the pioneer boot works, owned and managed by our own comrades; in insurance the Planet Collecting Society; in social recreation the Club and Institute Union is the most democratic body in the country. There is also the Co-operative Movement, whose defects can be remedied.[32]

The West Leeds branch, which had, in this spirit, set up a Socialist Supply Association to supply general provisions and goods cheaply, also ran a Sunday School and choirs, while 'the club is a centre for social life and fellowship, for intellectual, political and artistic development'. Thus, the BSP had some interest in direct control through co-operation, and there was a potential for this to be linked with the programme for the expansion of democratic municipal enterprise associated with the ILP. However, the overwhelming problem posed by nationalism and war in August 1914 froze any further coming together of Labour Party and BSP politics. When the war ended, a completely new configuration of politics on the left was brought about as a consequence of the 1917 Russian Revolution.[33]

A wide range of radical and revolutionary ideas and groups thus formed an important part of the political culture in Leeds between 1880 and 1914, but by the early years of the twentieth century the socialist and labour movement had defined its goals in terms of the conquest of political power through central and local government, with the dual purpose of promoting reforms of working-class conditions and of developing the function of the state towards a policy of general economic benevolence. This policy enabled Labour to consolidate and develop its powers in the period between the First and Second World Wars, when the West Yorkshire region became the 'Labour Heartland'.[34] The Labour Party replaced the Liberal Party as the alternative to the Conservatives. It formed two minority governments, in 1924 and 1929, and won, on average, 9 out of the 23 West Yorkshire parliamentary seats in the seven general elections which took place between 1918 and 1939. In 1945 Labour won 21 of the 23 West Yorkshire seats as the Attlee government came into power. Laybourn has summarized the appeal of the party well:

> The appeal of the Labour Party was basically a simple one. A civilised society aimed to generate work for all who needed it, and if this could

not be achieved adequate maintenance should be provided for those not in work. The conditions of decent health required urgent attention – adequate provision for medical services ... Reform of the educational system to provide a proper education for all irrespective of class was perhaps the highest priority of all. In international affairs, support for the League of Nations and the principles of collective security were seen as offering the best safeguards against war ...[35]

This is a fair acknowledgement of the efforts of those who worked for a civilized society, or who nourished the liberty tree, in the period covered by this book. It is unlikely that Maguire, who penned the appeal for a socialist Labour Party in 1887, and who died from poverty and tuberculosis only eight years later, would have disagreed with this assessment.

Notes

1. D. B. Foster, *Life Story* (Leeds, 1921), p. 27.
2. William Morris, in Edward Thompson, *William Morris, Romantic to Revolutionary* (London, 1977), p. 685.
3. D. Howell, *British Workers and the Independent Labour Party 1888–1906* (Manchester, 1983), p. 389.
4. Keith Laybourn, *The Rise of Labour: The British Labour Party 1890–1979* (London, 1988).
5. P. F. Clarke, *Lancashire and the New Liberalism* (Cambridge, 1971); T. Wilson *The Downfall of the Liberal Party 1914–1935* (London, 1966); R. Douglas 'Labour in Decline', in K. D. Brown (ed.), *Essays in Anti-Labour History* (Basingstoke, 1974).
6. K. O. Morgan, 'The New Liberalism and the Challenge of Labour: The Welsh Experience 1885–1929', in Brown (ed.) *Essays in Anti-Labour History;* A. W. Purdue, 'The Liberal and Labour Party in North East Politics', *International Review of Social History* I (1981).
7. D. Tanner, *Political Change and the Labour Party 1900–1918* (Cambridge, 1990).
8. *Ibid.*, p. 249.
9. *Ibid.*, p. 259.
10. Laybourn, *The Rise of Labour*, H. Pelling, *The Origins of the Labour Party* (London, 1954), and R. McKibbin, *The Evolution of the Labour Party 1910–1924* (Oxford, 1974), both argue that the rise of Labour was well established before the war.
11. P. Thompson, *Socialists, Liberals and Labour: The Struggle for London 1885–1914* (London, 1967).
12. See Laybourn, *The Rise of Labour*, p. 27. For other comparative studies on the ILP in Yorkshire see K. Laybourn and J. Reynolds, *Liberalism and the Rise of Labour, 1880–1914* (London, 1984); J. Reynolds and K. Laybourn, 'The Emergence of the Independent Labour Party in Bradford', *International Review of Social History* XX (1975); D. James, 'The Keighley ILP 1982–1900: Realising the Kingdom of Heaven', in J. A. Jowitt and

R. K. S. Taylor (eds), *Bradford 1890–1914: The Cradle of the ILP* (Leeds, 1980); R. B. Perks, 'Liberalism and the Challenge of Labour in West Yorkshire, 1885–1914, with special reference to Huddersfield', Ph.D. thesis (Huddersfield Polytechnic, 1985): M. D. Pugh, 'Yorkshire and the New Liberalism?' *Journal of Modern History* (1978).

13. Bill Lancaster, *Radicalism, Cooperation and Socialism: Leicester Working Class Politics 1860–1906* (Leicester, 1987).

14. *Ibid.*, p. xxii.

15. *Ibid.*

16. This discussion is based on J. Quail, *The Slow Burning Fuse* (London, 1978).

17. R. Rocker, *The London Years* (London, 1956).

18. D. B. Foster, *Life Story* (Leeds, 1921), p. 26.

19. *Ibid.*, p. 27.

20. B. Holton, *British Syndicalism, 1900–1914* (London, 1976).

21. See P. Mairet, *A. R. Orage: A Memoir* (London, 1936).

22. See W. Martin, *The New Age Under Orage* (London, 1967).

23. A. R. Orage, 'Politics for Craftsmen', *Contemporary Review* 91 (1907), pp. 782–94.

24. For an account of this see Edward Thompson, *William Morris, Romantic to Revolutionary* (London, 1977), p. 605 *passim*.

25. M. Crick, *The History of the Social Democratic Federation* (Keele, 1994).

26. *Ibid.*, pp. 214–15.

27. 'BSP Notes', *Leeds Weekly Citizen* (*LWC*), 13 January 1913.

28. For a history of the Workers' Union see R. Hyman, *The Workers' Union* (Oxford, 1971).

29. See J. E. Williams, 'The Leeds Corporation Strike in 1913', in A. Briggs and J. Saville (eds), *Essays in Labour History 1886–1923* (London, 1971).

30. See Holton, *British Syndicalism*.

31. LLRC, Executive Committee Minutes, 10 April 1913, and LLRC, General Committee Minutes, 17 April 1913.

32. *LWC*, 13 March 1914.

33. See W. Kendall, *The Revolutionary Movement in Britain* (London, 1969).

34. J. Reynolds and K. Laybourn, *Labour Heartland; A History of the Labour Party in West Yorkshire During the Inter-War Years 1918–1939* (Bradford, 1987).

35. *Ibid.*, p. 21.

Bibliography

Main sources and works are listed here. More detailed information can be gathered by following sources in the references at the end of each chapter. The Ph.D. thesis from which this book was developed (Woodhouse, 1982, see below) contains a comprehensive listing of sources.

Personal Papers and Collections

Edward Carpenter Collection, Sheffield City Library
Viscount Gladstone Papers, British Museum (Add. MSS. 46027–41)
George Howell Collection, Bishopsgate Institute
Webb Collection, English Local Government Papers, Vol. 256, LSE
John Lincoln Mahon: a collection of letters and newspaper cuttings in
    possession of John Mahon, Leatherhead
Alfred Mattison Collection, Brotherton Library, University of Leeds

Records of Political Parties and Labour Organizations

British Socialist Party, Papers, 1910–1914, LSE
ILP National Administrative Council Minutes, 1893–1909 and 1909–1932
    (Microfilm Record, University of Bradford Library)
Archives of the ILP: The Francis Johnson Correspondence, 1888–1950
    (Harvester Press Microfilm, 1980)
Archives of the Labour Party and the Labour Representation Com-
    mittee, Labour Party London
City of Leeds Labour Party, 1911–1931, Leeds City Archives
Leeds and District Trades Council, 1882–1914, Leeds City Archives
Socialist League Papers (correspondence of Maguire and Mahon, Octo-
    ber and November 1885), International Institute for Social His-
    tory, Amsterdam

Newspapers

Clarion (1891–1932)
Commonweal (1885–1894)
Forward (Leeds ILP; only 1898 and 1899 issues survive)
The Labour Leader (1893–1932)

Leeds Express
Leeds Mercury
Leeds Weekly Citizen (1911 to date)
Yorkshire Factory Times (1889–1926)

Articles

J. F. C. Harrison, 'Chartism in Leeds', in A.Briggs (ed.), *Chartist Studies* (London, 1959)

J. Hill, 'The Early ILP in Manchester and Salford', *International Review of Social History* XXVI (1981)

J. A. Jowitt and K. Laybourn, 'War and Socialism: The Experience of the Bradford Independent Labour Party 1914–1918', *Journal of Regional and Local Studies* 4, 2 (1984)

K. O. Morgan, 'The New Liberalism and the Challenge of Labour: The Welsh Experience 1885–1929', in Brown (ed.) *Essays in Anti-Labour History* (London, 1985)

M. D. Pugh, 'Yorkshire and the New Liberalism?', *Journal of Modern History* (1978)

A. W. Purdue, 'The Liberal and Labour Party in North East Politics', *International Review of Social History* I (1981)

J. Reynolds and K. Laybourn, 'The Emergence of the Independent Labour Party in Bradford', *International Review of Social History* XX (1975)

D. Rubinstein, 'The Independent Labour Party and the Yorkshire Miners: The Barnsley By-Election of 1897', *International Review of Social History* XXIII (1978)

M. Savage, 'The Rise of the Labour Party in Local Perspective', *The Journal of Regional and Local Studies* 10 (1990)

E. P. Thompson, 'Homage to Tom Maguire', in A. Briggs and J. Saville (eds) *Essays in Labour History* (London, 1960)

Books

J. M. Bellamy and J. Saville (eds), *Dictionary of Labour Biography*, 9 Vols. (Basingstoke, 1972–1993)

F. Brockway, *Socialism over Sixty Years* (London, 1946)

K. D. Brown (ed.), *The First Labour Party 1906–1914* (London, 1985)

E. Carpenter, *My Days and Dreams* (London, 1916)

D. Clark, *Colne Valley: Radicalism to Socialism; the Portrait of a Northern Constituency in the Formative Years of the Labour Party 1890–1910* (London, 1981)

P. F. Clarke, *Lancashire and the New Liberalism* (Cambridge, 1971)

M. Crick, *The History of the Social Democratic Federation* (Keele, 1994)

I. O. Ford (ed.), *Tom Maguire, A Remembrance: being selections from the prose and verse writings of a socialist pioneer* (Manchester, 1895)

D. B. Foster, *Life Story* (Leeds, 1921)

D. Fraser (ed.), *A History of Modern Leeds* (Manchester, 1980)

M. Gawthorpe, *Up Hill to Holloway* (Penobscot/Traversity Press, 1962)

J. F. C. Harrison, *Social Reform in Victorian Leeds: The Work of James Hole 1820–1895* (Leeds, 1954)

D. Howell, *British Workers and the Independent Labour Party 1888–1906* (Manchester, 1983)

D. James, T. Jowitt and K. Laybourn (eds), *The Centennial History of the Independent Labour Party* (Halifax, 1992)

J. A. Jowitt and R.K.S. Taylor (eds), *Bradford 1890–1914: The Cradle of the ILP* (Leeds, 1980)

B. Lancaster, *Radicalism, Cooperation and Socialism: Leicester Working Class Politics 1860–1906* (Leicester, 1987)

K. Laybourn and J. Reynolds, *Liberalism and the Rise of Labour, 1880–1914* (London, 1984)

K. Laybourn, *The Rise of Labour: The British Labour Party 1890–1979* (London, 1988)

K. Laybourn and D. James (eds), *'The Rising Sun of Socialism': The Independent Labour Party in the Textile District of the West Riding of Yorkshire between 1880 and 1914* (West Yorkshire Archive Service, 1991)

H. Pelling, *The Origins of the Labour Party* (London, 1954)

R. McKibbon, *The Evolution of the Labour Party 1910–1914* (Oxford, 1974)

J. Reynolds and K. Laybourn, *Labour Heartland* (Bradford, 1987)

S. Rowbotham and J. Weekes, *Socialism and the New Life* (London, 1977)

L. Smith, *Religion and the Rise of Socialism* (Keele, 1993)

T. Steele, *Alfred Orage and the Leeds Arts Club 1893–1923* (Aldershot, 1990)

D. Tanner *Political Change and the Labour Party* (Cambridge, 1990)

E. P. Thompson, *William Morris, Romantic to Revolutionary* (London, 1977)

T. Wilson, *The Downfall of the Liberal Party 1914–1935* (London 1966)

Unpublished theses

J. Buckman, 'The Economic and Social History of Alien Immigrants to Leeds 1880–1914', Ph.D. thesis (University of Strathclyde, 1968)

D. Jones, 'The Liberal Press and the Rise of Labour: A Study with particular reference to Leeds and Bradford, 1850–1895', Ph.D. thesis (University of Leeds, 1973)

R.B. Perks, 'Liberalism and the Challenge of Labour in West Yorkshire, 1885–1914, with special reference to Huddersfield', Ph.D. thesis (Huddersfield Polytechnic, 1985)

A. Roberts, 'The Liberal Party in West Yorkshire 1885–1895: with an epilogue 1885–1914', Ph.D. thesis (University of Leeds, 1979)

T. Woodhouse, 'A Political History of the Leeds Labour Movement, 1880–1914', Ph.D. thesis (University of Leeds, 1982)

Chronology

1855   Leeds Chartists form the Leeds Advanced Liberal Party
1860   Leeds Working Men's Parliamentary Reform Association
1860   Leeds Trades Council formed
1883   Formation of the Social Democratic Federation
1884   Third Parliamentary Reform Act
1884   Formation of Leeds branch of the Social Democratic Federation (September)
1884   Formation of the Socialist League (December)
1885   Formation of Leeds branch of the Socialist League, February
1887   Tom Maguire of the Socialist League in Leeds issues a handbill calling for the formation a Socialist Labour Party
1889   London dockers' strike and municipal gas strike leading to the formation of new unions of the unskilled (Gasworkers and General Labourers' Union)
1890   Labour Electoral League formed (first of two precursors to the Leeds ILP)
1891   William Cockayne of the GGLU fights East Hunslet in the first municipal election fought by an independent labour candidate in Leeds
1892   Leeds Trades and Labour Council Labour Electoral Union formed (second precursor to the Leeds ILP)
1892   East Hunslet Independent Labour Party formed, becomes Leeds ILP (October/November 1892)
1893   ILP Foundation Conference at Bradford (January)
1894   Leeds Central ILP Club opened by Keir Hardie (October)
1895   Arthur Shaw is first ILP member to become president of the Trades Council, and first ILP candidate to run in a parliamentary election in Leeds (South Leeds). Tom Maguire dies
1896   Leeds SDF branch re-formed at Armley (possibly 1894?)
1900   Labour Representation Committee formed, Memorial Hall London (27 February).
1900   Leeds Trades Council affiliates to Labour Representation Committee (June)

1901   Taff Vale Judgement awards damages against Amalgamated
         Society of Railway Servants for losses incurred in a strike. Pro-
         tection for trade unions restored by an Act of 1906
1903   John Buckle of NUBSO wins first Labour Party (LLRC)
         seat on Leeds City Council, at New Wortley. Informal
         Gladstone–MacDonald agreement for limited collaboration in
         general election of 1906
1906   The Labour Representation Committee nationally changes its
         name to the Labour Party. James O'Grady wins East Leeds in
         general election of 1906: first Labour parliamentary victory in
         Leeds
1909   The Osborne Judgement prevents trade unions from levying
         funds for the Labour Party
1911   Socialist Unity Conference Manchester and formation of Brit-
         ish Socialist Party
1913   Trade Union Act allows unions to ballot members for support
         of a political levy
1914   Leeds Labour Representation Committee renamed as Leeds
         Labour Party. Labour Party has more elected councillors than
         Liberal Party

Index